THE GOETHEANUM

RUDOLF STEINER'S ARCHITECTURAL IMPULSE

HAGEN BIESANTZ – ARNE KLINGBORG

with contributions by

ÅKE FANT, REX RAAB, NIKOLAUS RUFF

translated by Jean Schmid

RUDOLF STEINER PRESS
LONDON

Photographs
D. Cole, London
E. Gmelin, Dornach
H. Gross, Basle
Heydebrand-Osthoff Studio, Dornach
O. Rietmann, St. Gallen
W. Roggenkamp, Süderfahrenstedt
J. Wilkes, Forest Row

Layout
Arne Klingborg

Copyright (illustrations)
Philosophisch-Anthroposophischer Verlag,
Dornach, Switzerland, 1978.
Copyright (text)
Rudolf Steiner Press, London 1979.

Set by Yale Press, London
Made and printed by Bigwood and Staple Ltd, Bridgwater

ISBN 0 85440 355 8

CONTENTS

Preface 7

On the Way to a New Style in Architecture 9

The First Goetheanum 21

The Second Goetheanum 55

Rudolf Steiner's Aesthetics 83

Rudolf Steiner's Architectural Impulse in
    Modern Architectural History 91

The Goetheanum in Professional Literature .. 99

Rudolf Steiner's Continuing Architectural
    Impulse 105

The Practising Architect and the School
    for Spiritual Science at the Goetheanum 109

Index of Architects 110

The Dornach Building Chronicle 124

Bibliography 125

List of Illustrations 128

Annotations 130

All marginal texts are quoted from Rudolf Steiner's lectures.
For sources, see p.127

PREFACE

The second Goetheanum was opened fifty years ago. Its organic living forms were the fruits of an architectural impulse which Rudolf Steiner had been able to develop on Swiss soil since 1913. Here a new architectural movement found its beginnings, whose growth is now demonstrated by representative buildings all over the world.

As mechanized construction gains ground, the need also grows for a living 'human' architecture. This accounts for the attention that has been bestowed upon the Goetheanum in recent professional literature. Architects and structural engineers are beginning to discover Rudolf Steiner's architectural language of forms and to derive stimulation from it for their own activities. Rex Raab has described this development in his book *Eloquent Concrete*.

This attention which the Goetheanum is now receiving from the professional world corresponds with a waxing interest on the part of the general public. Modern man's longing for a more 'human' architecture is directed towards organic building forms. To meet this need, an exhibition was mounted at the Goetheanum – from 8 July to 6 October 1978 – which documents the genesis of the building and its effects on contemporary architectural activity. It demonstrates that the Goetheanum is not an isolated phenomenon in the architectural history of our time, but that it represents a decisive contribution towards the realization of such a living, humanized architecture. The following chapters aim to serve a more intensive study of what was displayed in the exhibition.

The plans and models for the general development of the Goetheanum site cannot be taken into consideration at this juncture. The Goetheanum as seat of the Free School of Spiritual Science is the central building of a complex which has not yet been fully exploited. It is surrounded by ancillary buildings serving scientific and artistic work and student-training purposes. The considerable expansion of the college activities has given rise to a shortage of space that urgently calls for additional buildings on the site. Planning has now been in progress for several years. This has to proceed from Rudolf Steiner's original conception and is thus confronted with interesting artistic tasks, whose solution cannot be discussed until after the work has been completed.

The idea for the present publication originated with Arne Klingborg, who attended to its actual design, chose the marginal texts and, together with Åke Fant, compiled a list of Rudolf Steiner's architectural adherents. The main text was written by Hagen Biesantz, with supplementary contributions by Åke Fant, Rex Raab and Nikolaus Ruff.

The illustrations of the first Goetheanum are drawn from the Heydebrand-Osthoff-Studio, Dornach, and from Oscar Rietmann, St. Gallen. The photographs taken during the construction of the second Goetheanum are all by the photographer Oscar Rietmann, without whose life-work a documentation of the building activity on the Dornach hill would not have been possible. We are particularly indebted to Emil Gmelin, Dornach, and Hans Gross, Basle, for the more recent photographs of the second Goetheanum.

With their information and help in compiling the material, Emil Estermann and Waldemar Kumm, both active at the Goetheanum in Dornach, have been of invaluable assistance. Frau Ruth Savin of the Philosophisch-Anthroposophischer Verlag made the book's publication possible at very short notice. The Iona Foundation in Amsterdam kindly supported the preliminary scientific research. We extend our cordial thanks to all those mentioned above and to their colleagues.

Goetheanum, June 1978   Hagen Biesantz
                                          Arne Klingborg

ON THE WAY TO A NEW STYLE IN ARCHITECTURE

Hagen Biesantz

It is 1907. The 'Revolution of Modern Art' is in full swing. The new style in architecture (Art Nouveau – Jugendstil) has made its mark in the cultural centres of the western world and painters and sculptors are striving to attain new forms of artistic expression. Colour and form are to be released from the constraints imposed by a rational approach to art and become independent expressions of a newly awakened spirituality.

Little noticed amidst this universal uprising is a 46-year-old scientist, who a few years later is to emerge as a significant architect, but whose contribution to art has previously only been in the field of literature and, occasionally, the theatre, in the role of producer.

This scientist was Rudolf Steiner, General Secretary of the German Section of the Theosophical Society. Up to the turn of the century known and respected as philosopher and editor of Goethe's works on natural science, Steiner began in 1902 to publish the results of his spiritual research and introduced a group of students to the research methods he had developed. By 1907, the Section of the Theosophical Society which he conducted had gained such strength that this society's annual congress could be held on German-speaking territory, in Munich.

> The Munich Congress was intended to bear witness to something which I have again and again stressed with regard to our theosophical impulse. It was to show that Theosophy is not only a matter of personal brooding and introspection. Theosophy should make an impact on practical life, should be a matter of education, a matter of involvement in all branches of practical existence. Only those who have a deeper understanding and a more profound conception of the essential impulses of Theosophy can know today what possibilities this Theosophy will have to offer in the future.
> Berlin, 12 June 1907

The Munich Congress

The 'Munich Congress' built a first bridge between spiritual research and art. This event was as revolutionary for those interested in spiritual investigation as modern art then was for the prevalent bourgeois culture. Following oriental wisdom, the members of the Theosophical Society were accustomed to regarding the world about them as a world of appearance (Maya), – an approach which did not call for an active relationship to art. Rudolf Steiner, whose spiritual investigations proceeded from western Christianity, saw the spirit's expression in the material world. Schiller's concept of 'fair appearance' provided him with a key to discovering art as a higher reality within the reality of nature. Artistic creation was thus a consequence of his spiritual research and signified the initial step on the way leading to the revelation of the spirit in the world of the senses. It was therefore a continuation of his previous

Seventh planetary seal (Venus Seal) – Sketch by Rudolf Steiner 1907

The Munich Congress Hall with the painted seals and columns in 1907. From left to right in first row: 2nd, Annie Besant; 4th, Marie von Sivers (Steiner); 5th, Rudolf Steiner; 7th, Sophie Stinde

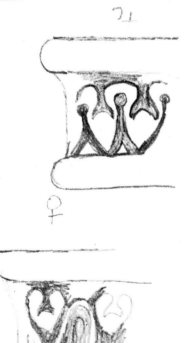

Jupiter and Venus Capitals of the painted columns in the Munich Congress Hall. Sketches by Rudolf Steiner 1907

research and teaching activity that he himself made a move to create the artistic surroundings for the Munich Congress.[1]

The given circumstances were such that the artistic arrangement had to remain limited to the interior decoration of a rented hall. However, even here it was evident that the artistic design was intended for an actual building. The main element of the hall's decoration consisted of a row of seven columns painted on tall, rectangular boards, which alternated with painted *tondi* (circular pictures) of the seven apocalyptic seals. The columns, which really have to be conceived in the round, corresponded in the forms of their capitals to particular planetary stages in the earth's development. The (spiritual) element of reality of these sculpturally treated architectural works of art was contained in their *sequence*. The resulting transformation from capital to capital at the same time represented something quite new in the history of modern art. The form of each capital is different from the preceding and subsequent form. The transition from one form to the next is however quite in accordance with law. Just as the plant grows and is transformed from bud and leaf to blossom and fruit and is germinated again from its seeds and roots, the row of capitals evinces forms growing out of one another. The principle of metamorphosis, which was discovered by Goethe in relationship to plant growth, is here realized for the first time in fine art. Thus, even before the efforts of Nouveau Art to create an organic style in architec-

10

ture had to yield to the rise of functionalism, a decisive break-through had been achieved, where all previous attempts in this field had failed. The organic style in architecture had only now found its appropriate principle, metamorphosis. If it had then been able to find general recognition, the further development of architecture in our century would certainly have progressed quite differently. An organic style of architecture without the principle of metamorphosis cannot flourish; it is like a plant whose growth is stunted. The validity of such a style is connected with the very laws of plant growth.

The Model Building in Malsch

That as early as 1907 Rudolf Steiner aimed to make public the artistic impulse resulting from an experience of spiritual reality, is indicated in a report on the Munich Congress, which he gave in Berlin on 12 June of that year: 'Seven column *motifs* heralded the age when buildings can also be dedicated to theosophy.'[2] Yet the realization of such an intention depended upon other people accepting this idea out of their own initiative. As spiritual teacher, Steiner had to avoid influencing his students' decisions of will in any way. Fortunately, 21-year-old E. A. Karl Stockmeyer from Malsch, near Karlsruhe in south-west Germany, was amongst the youngest participants of the congress. The artistic arrangement of the congress hall had deeply impressed him. The painted columns had particularly stimulated his imagination. 'The column paint-

The Malsch Model Building – Interior after completion (by A. v. Baravalle) – View eastwards from the entrance

Jupiter Column painted on a board by Karl Stahl (painter) (in accordance with a folder published by Rudolf Steiner in 1907)

The second seal in the Munich Congress Hall – Sketch by Rudolf Steiner 1907

ings standing freely without entablature and ceiling, with the round pictures hanging between them on the red wall, represented a challenge to conceive a structure which would incorporate the columns as supporting elements.'[3] In the summer of 1908, Stockmeyer asked Rudolf Steiner about the architecture appertaining to the columns. In reply, he was told to imagine an elliptical space enclosed on both sides by a row of seven columns. These were to support a cupola in the form of a triaxial ellipsoid, whose main axis was to run from west to east. There was to be an ambulatory behind the columns and an elliptical wall was to encompass the whole externally.[3] A crypt-like interior was thus initially conceived, whose elliptical form nevertheless differed fundamentally from earlier architectural forms. This form already revealed what was later to be accomplished in the first Goetheanum in the form of the double-domed building: the establishment of an organic relationship between the longitudinal character of an axial building (basilica, cathedral) and the circular character of a central building (Pantheon). The importance of this step for modern architectural experience will be discussed later in connection with the first Goetheanum (p.39 ff).

In his home town of Malsch, Stockmeyer first set about erecting a *model building* with columns 0.87 metres high (total height 1.74 metres) and dimensions on plan of approximately 2.5 : 3.5 metres. So that the interior would be spacious enough to accommodate smaller meetings (up to 24 people), the floor was sunk below the level of the column bases. In April 1909, Rudolf Steiner laid the foundation stone of this building. The topping-out ceremony did not take place until later.[4]

A true understanding of the matter cannot be reached if observation of the forms is based solely on intellectual explanation. It is necessary to contemplate the forms with true *artistic feeling,* it is necessary to allow the capitals to work on one purely as *form.* Those who do not take this into account will believe that they are viewing nothing more than allegories, or at best symbols. They would thus have misunderstood everything.
October 1907

Lecture Hall in the Stuttgart House of the Anthroposophical Society, Landhausstrasse 70

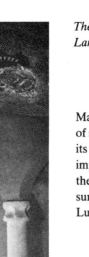

The colonnade in the Stuttgart House, Landhausstrasse 70

The Interior Space in Stuttgart

What had taken place on a modest scale in Malsch, unnoticed by the cultural world, was soon to prove the germ of an architectural impulse which was gradually to assert itself more and more. Like a seed entrusted to the soil at the right time, the Malsch model germinated just before the frost period in modern art, classified as 'Abstract Art', 'Functionalism', 'neue Sachlichkeit' (New Objectivity), etc., really set in. In 1909-10, the first non-representational compositions by Kandinsky, Arthur Dove (U.S.A.) and others came into being and in 1911 Gropius designed the Fagus Works, which are alienated from the organic architectural impulse. Gropius, colleague of the Jugendstil architect, Peter Behrens, draws as it were the consequence from the fact that the organic Nouveau Art style in architecture had proved incapable of penetrating material reality, as it could have through metamorphosis, and, wrestling for artistic truth, turns to a technological functionalism devoid of any expression of organic growth. A public confrontation of the Fagus Works with an edifice arising out of consistent organic architectural incentives ought to have taken place at this time. This might have been made possible by the members of the Theosophical Society in Stuttgart, who in 1910 had established a fund towards the erection of their own premises. Yet such were the circumstances that the exterior forms of the resulting building (Landhausstrasse 70) were not inspired by the new architectural impulse. A continuation of the Malsch impulse had to be concentrated on the interior, particularly on a meeting room in the basement, where the Malsch model was carried out on a larger scale. What the Munich Congress had merely intimated here became architectural reality. A

Man can only experience true harmony of soul where what his soul knows to be its most valuable thoughts, feelings and impulses are mirrored for his senses in the forms, colours and so on of his surroundings.
Lucifer-Gnosis, No. 34, 1907

An opaque paint on a wall is different from a paint which is translucent. When we observe translucent colour surrounding us here we must say: Just as through the colour of an opaque painted wall we enter into a relationship with certain beings, so through a translucent, shining colour on a wall we enter into a relationship with other beings. The beings we relate to through the opaque painted wall are in the first instance spread out in space but have actually nothing to do with the three kingdoms of nature, the mineral, plant and animal kingdoms. But through translucent colours we enter into a relationship with those beings who are directly occupied with bringing into being the objects of the three natural kingdoms. In particular if we look through translucent red on the wall we relate to beings of a quite special kind within our natural kingdoms. When translucent red makes a kind of window through which we can look clairvoyantly into the kingdoms of nature, we meet with beings whose work brings out the best forces for the future of our earth existence. They must be there within the kingdoms of nature so that for man inner forces can grow which make him ever more chaste in his blood, that is in his life of passions. And when we regard the kingdoms of nature it this way, then we see the beings who warn us, also in our unconscious, the beings who more than any others challenge us to make progress in the purification of our passions.
Stuttgart, 15 October 1911

We have to realise that so long as we are compelled to hold our meetings in halls whose forms belong to a declining culture, our work will unavoidably also more or less share the fate of all that is caught up in this decline. The spiritual stream will not be able to bring forth the new culture in the way this should happen if it is not allowed the possibility of working right into the physical, even into the process of giving form to the very walls that surround us. Spiritual life will work differently when it is enabled to flow from rooms the forms and measurements of which spring from spiritual science.

Stuttgart, 3 January 1911

confrontation of the exterior of the Fagus Works with the interior of this Stuttgart hall serves to depict the cross-roads at which the architecture of our century had arrived in the years before the First World War – a stereometric functionalism or an organic, living style of architecture. The fact that the latter, like an Early Christian catacomb, still remained concealed from the public eye, whilst unorganic functionalism was boldly exhibited, appears as a symptom of that cultural disease which was to spread throughout the world as the century progressed: aesthetic apathy in the face of the living building form. Rudolf Steiner wanted to oppose this development when, in November 1911, he founded a 'Society for Theosophical Style in Art' in the newly completed Stuttgart premises.[5] It was to be its task to create the spiritual prerequisites for a public engagement in artistic and social life, which would be able to unfold its own initiatives even without Rudolf Steiner's assistance. The attempt failed. One consequence of its failure may be seen in the fact that in 1935 the Stuttgart building fell a victim to the political actions undertaken against the spiritual movement inaugurated by Rudolf Steiner. The hall was later destroyed. Only the sandstone columns, which are now in the gardens of the Friedrich Husemann Clinic at Wiesneck near Freiburg in Breisgau, were saved.

'Cosmic Midnight' in Rudolf Steiner's Mystery Drama 'The Soul's Awakening' – Sketch by Hans Kühn-Honegger after the premier in Munich in 1913

The Munich Project (Johannes Building)

Whilst the Stuttgart premises were still under construction, plans were already being made to erect a theatre in Munich. Since 1907, Rudolf Steiner's own Mystery Plays were being produced for annual congresses there, as the 'Sacred Drama of Eleusis' by Eduard Schuré had been in 1907. The performances of these dramas had to take place in rented theatres, whose architectural style by no means corresponded with the content and style of the stage art. Carl Schmid-Curtius, architect of the Stuttgart building, was commissioned to work out the plans for the Munich Project. As regards the directions he had been given, the architect later commented:[6] 'All that was passed on to me was Rudolf Steiner's indication that two interpenetrating circles might comprise auditorium and stage.' This more than scanty information nevertheless implied a decisive turning-point in architectural design liberated from all traditional confinements. The concept of the twin-domed building with two interpenetrating cupola segments was born. As Rudolf Steiner himself stated, he had already conceived this idea in 1908, although he did not mention it until 1909 in a private conversation (with Ernst Uehli) and then again in 1911, when Alexander Strakosch asked him for particulars concerning the Munich project (see Kemper).[6] It is important

Maria and Johannes Thomasius in Rudolf Steiner's Mystery Drama 'The Portal of Initiation' – Maria: Marie v. Sivers (Steiner); Johannes: Mieta Pyle (Waller)

'Ahriman's Realm' in Rudolf Steiner's Mystery Drama 'The Guardian of the Threshold' – Sketch by Hans Kühn-Honegger after the premier in Munich in 1913

After many years during which I myself and others had been disseminating this spiritual science in many different countries and places by giving lectures and speaking about its ideas and ideals, the inner necessity became apparent round about the years 1909 or 1910 for a method, other than that of the mere thoughts and words, of revealing and passing on to the souls of our fellow men what is meant by spiritual science. Thus it came about that performances were given – at first in Munich – of a series of mystery dramas which I had written and which were intended to show in pictures and scenes the content about which anthroposophical spiritual science, in accordance with its very nature, must speak.

Berne, 29 June 1921

to note that the idea of 'two interpenetrating circles' was conceived at the same time as Stockmeyer's attention was drawn to the ellipsoid form of the Malsch model building. The double-domed structure thus ideally represents the same principle as Stockmeyer later recognized in the triaxial ellipsoid: to merge 'the rectilinear tendency of the temples of antiquity with the rotary tendencies of the rotunda and dome by the homogenous elliptical form.'[7] The ellipsoid was thus an intermediary stage on the way leading to the double-cupolaed edifice. The building planned for Munich ought to have become the first monument to demonstrate this new concept of spatial arrangement. Then the project, which had already assumed definite shape in 1911, met with opposition from the building authorities, and foundered. Its execution was delayed for two years, when it could finally be commenced on Swiss soil in Dornach, near Basle. Munich, City of the Arts, remained without an example of the new organic architectural impulse which had originally been intended for it. It may appear as a symptom of the tragedy which was to befall Central European cultural life, that the 'House of German Art' later arose in this city and all contemporary artistic aspiration was discredited as 'degenerate art'.

The Essence of the Double Cupola

Before we proceed to the first Goetheanum Building in Dornach, reference should first be made to the architectural experience conveyed by a double cupolaed building. This was the aim of the Munich project. The execution of this building concept had thus already been envisaged for the year 1911. Ever since larger interior spaces have been created to

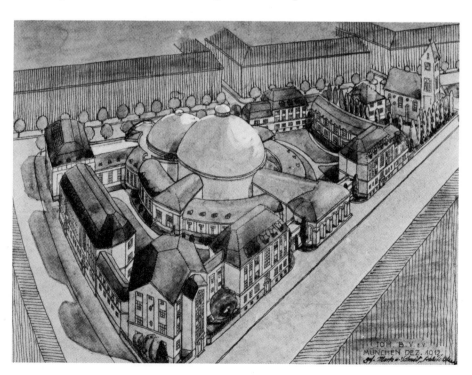

Model sketch of the Johannes Building in Munich – 1912

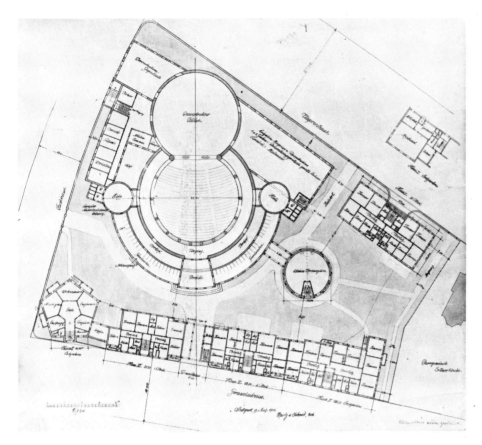

Ground plan of the Johannes Building in Munich 1912/13

For when it comes to the question of whether Anthroposophy will find a wider response in the world today, so much more depends upon deed than upon any answer expressed in words or thoughts. Very much depends, too, upon everyone contributing, as far as he can, to the aim of the Johannes Building Association, which is, with such understanding, taking its place in the evolution of mankind.
Berlin, 12 December 1911

In comparison with the living reality, spiritual science as an explanation of the universe is just as abstract and barren as is a commentary in comparison with an actual work of art.
Berlin, 12 December 1911

serve man's spiritual needs and celebrations, the contrasting forms of the basilican or longitudinal building and the central building can be recognized. The first large meeting place of this kind was the Telesterion for the Mystery Dramas in Eleusis near Athens, which the architect, Iktinos, converted to a square-shaped central building in the 5th century B.C.[8] This was followed by the truly circular or domed buildings of the Pantheon in Rome (2nd century A.D.), the Early Christian baptistries and mausoleums, and later the domed churches of Eastern Christianity. Aisled buildings for ritual assemblies developed from the original form of the Greek temple (which, as the House of God, was not a meeting place), to emerge in basilicas and cathedrals as the determining form for Western Christianity. If an attempt is made to describe the experience of space in an aisled church, essential appears to be the fact that the person entering the church is induced to move, as he experiences the distance between his location and the object of his aspiration, the altar. The rows of columns running up to the apse on both sides indicate the way and summon him to move in the same direction. On the other hand, the central building mediates a sense of rest. Instinctively, the visitor feels himself to be standing at its centre and thus at an equal distance from all points on the same level of the circumference (walls and cupola). He does not sense the urge to move away from his central position. All distances between himself and the building compensate one another. The

Sketches by Rudolf Steiner of the columns and architraves in the large rotunda – 1913

edifice claims rest, not movement. (The 'rotary tendency' of domed buildings alluded to by Stockmeyer has to be conceived by an act of will. It was not experienced involuntarily). Thus it may be asserted that the central building emanates peace and security in the harmony of a cosmos, whereas the axial building provokes activity and movement. Common to both is that they each exact the given experience, i.e. up to a certain extent extort it. However, the double domed building enables a new experience of freedom in spatial perception, which is generated when the rotunda and cupola effect is brought into a fluctuating equilibrium with the longitudinal axis effect. Upon entering the larger rotunda with its cupola, the visitor experiences the repose and harmony of the almost complete rotunda in which he finds himself, but at the same time he feels himself to be standing on a longitudinal axis which has arisen from the

Sketches by Rudolf Steiner of the columns and architraves in the small rotunda – 1913

extension of the larger cupola's diameter into the smaller cupola. The prospect into the open small cupola makes the distance between the visitor and the culminating niche in the rear wall of the small cupola appear such, that movement towards it would be the natural consequence of this directional experience. Thus the visitor is himself able to determine which of the two possible experiences – rest or movement – is to take precedence. He is able to shift from one experience to the other by the slightest stimulation of will. What the building itself imparts to the visitor is the feeling of not being committed; it conveys the sense of equilibrium between rest and movement and the freedom of himself being able to give spatial experience its direction. *The double domed building conveys the spatial experience of the human being awakened to individual freedom.*

Rudolf Steiner with a model of the first Goetheanum – 1914

Rudolf Steiner's interior model of the first Goetheanum – 1913

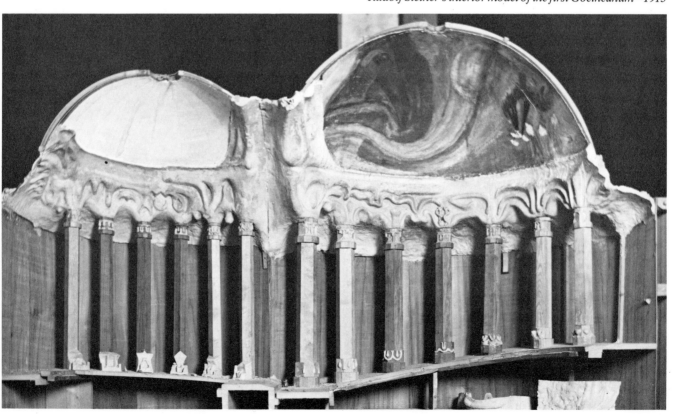

THE FIRST GOETHEANUM

Hagen Biesantz

After the principle of metamorphosis had been introduced into architecture by the Munich Congress (1907) and the variable equilibrium of spatial experience by the Johannes Building Project (1911), the possibility of executing the proposed building finally presented itself in Dornach, near Basle, where Rudolf Steiner had been offered the donation of a large plot of land. As this was situated on an elevated project at the foot of the Jura mountains, more importance had to be attributed to the exterior design from the outset than had been the case with the previous projects, which had been subordinated to urban conditions. A building had to be created whose exterior also indicated its interior design. On 20 September 1913, Rudolf Steiner laid the foundation stone and by 1 April 1914 the topping-out ceremony took place.

Organically Plastic Architecture

In the meantime Rudolf Steiner had been working on the final models for the interior and exterior design of the edifice.[9] As had been the case with the maquette, everything was first developed plastically. The forms did not arise at the drawing board but were moulded in plasticine and wax by his creative hand. The model for the interior, which was completed by the end of January 1914, represents a unique monument in architectural history. (This model is now at the Goetheanum in the anteroom leading to the carved sculptural 'Group'.) It illustrates the direction which the architectural impulse inaugurated in Munich in 1907 was really to take. Not merely an architectural enlivenment seeking expression in undulating lines (Nouveau Art), but rather an organically plastic structure had been created. In this, structural sculpture, which had previously only been appended to the architectural form as capitals, architraves, etc., now emerged as the creative element imbuing the architecture itself. Moreover, Rudolf Steiner designed a statue executed in wood and 9½ metres high for the culminating intercolumnar space of the small rotunda. Its motif, forms and proportions illustrated as it were the whole gesture of the architecture (particularly the element of equilibrium). But not only had architecture and sculpture been united. Painting was also fully integrated. The motifs for the paintings in the domes were developed out of great streams of colour flooding the interior surfaces to

For in our building the endeavour has been made to put aside everything of a personal nature, to represent in every line and every form not what flows from this individual personal nature but what the spiritual worlds reveal when we try to express world happenings in forms in order that men may be able to feel the meaning and significance of these happenings.
Dornach, 18 October 1914

p. 21 (2)

Look at the forms of our building: Everywhere the straight line is led over into the curve, balance is sought; everywhere the endeavour is made to melt what has become frozen, so that it may flow again, rest is everywhere created within movement and is then again caused to move. This is what is so spiritual about our building.
Dornach, 21 September 1918

Over and above the cultivation of spiritual science as a body of ideas and ideals, we sense that this spiritual science, poured livingly into the souls of men, demands an environment that differs from the one which today's dying culture has to offer.
Dornach, 26 July 1914

relate with the modelled sweep of the architraves. Likewise, light entering from without was incorporated in the artistic conception by coloured glass windows, which, in the colour sequence of green, blue, violet and pink, immersed the large rotunda in an atmosphere of iridescent colour. (The smaller rotunda, which was conceived as a stage, was without windows.) The prints recently published by Albert von Baravalle, the architect, convey an impression of this coloured light effect. For the window motifs Rudolf Steiner invented a new glass engraving technique.[10]

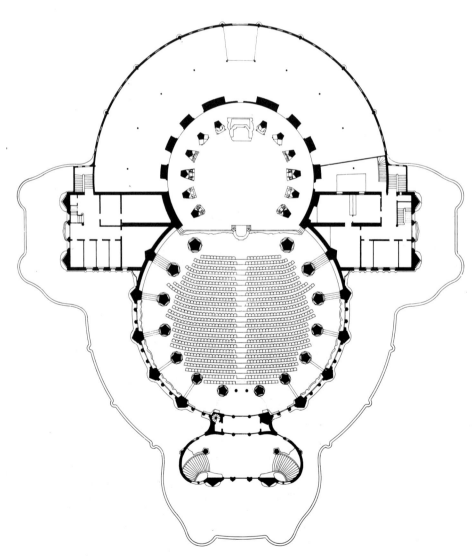

Right: Ground plan of the first Goetheanum

Far right: Interior model of the first Goetheanum – Design by Rudolf Steiner

The Total Work of Art

In the combined action of the arts, as it is manifested in the interior design of the first Goetheanum, a further aim of the Nouveau Art impulse became reality for the first time: the integrated total work of art. What was not called for publicly until 1919 in Gropius' 'Bauhaus' Manifesto and has since often been regarded as the artistic principle of the 'Bauhaus', was in reality an endeavour originating in the artistic revolution before the turn of the century.[11] Yet, as in the case of the organic architectural style, this intention was also not carried out to its last consequence. Not until the Goetheanum project was initiated, did an all-embracing architectural concept avail itself of all forms of art, which were together to create the organism which is in the fullest sense a total work of art. At the time the 'Bauhaus' proclaimed the original endeavour of Nouveau Art as a challenge for the future, its aims had already become a reality of the present. The Goetheanum building was standing in the centre of Europe, for all to see.

Rudolf Steiner on the speaker's rostrum in the carpenters' shop (lecture room during the building)

Working in Community

A further ideal of modern art was realized as the execution of the interior progressed – a working community. Originally a working party of artists (Builders' Corporation principle), it was extended at the Goetheanum to include the participation of unskilled assistants. From many European countries and overseas, people hurried to Switzerland, eager to help in the construction of the new edifice. They were all given a task at the Goetheanum, and some were even able to work artistically (particularly as wood-carvers). Rudolf Steiner himself initiated them in their new activities and demonstrated the skills required. The idealism of this active community was such that even during the First World War subjects from seventeen nations involved in the struggle worked together at the Goetheanum, whilst in neighbouring Alsace their countrymen fought embittered battles.

Wood-carving for the first Goetheanum

Audience in the carpenters' shop during a lecture

Wood-carving in the first Goetheanum – in the foreground: Saturn Column

Right: Members of the architects' office during the building period – right: Carl Schmid-Curtius; left: Ernst Aisenpreis

Opposite Page:
Top left: Engraving of the coloured glass windows for the first Goetheanum (in the Glass Studio)

Top right: Blue window – Design by Rudolf Steiner

Bottom: The 'Glass Studio' where the glass windows were engraved

Above and below: The first Goetheanum under construction – 10 February 1914

Elements of Style

What had originated in the original impulse in Munich as interior form now had to find its equivalent in the exterior form of the building as well. As the whole construction was of timber (on a concrete base), the possibility also existed of shaping the exterior walls plastically. According to Rudolf Steiner's conception, the plastic forms were to grow out of the walls. In this way the walls, which in the interior were characterized rather by forms recessed in character, would collectively create an impression of mobility, also of being penetrable.[12] In this artistically created 'etheric wall', as seen from outside, the organic forces can be experienced as bringing forth living forms, whereas from the inside they appear to the practised eye to recede or become 'transparent'.[13] That this treatment of the walls answers a spiritual need of modern man becomes evident, if one bears in mind, how subsequent 'Bauhaus' architecture attempted to come to terms with this requirement by replacing solid walls with glass, thus creating a substitute for the artistically conjured 'transparency' (cp. Farnsworth House in Illinois, U.S.A., by Mies van der Rohe). A further essential element in the treatment of the elevations is the way in which the shapes in relief are formed by the relationships of force at play in support and load. Whilst the 'Bauhaus' tendency in

modern architecture removed the contrasting expression of support and load and mere addition of stereometrical units predominated,[14] an attempt is made at the Goetheanum to trace and make visible in every detail the forces and their relationships inherent in the building.[12] This gives rise to new forms not only on the pilasters at the entrances and windows but also on the columns and piers in the interior. Of these, the supports of the imposing concrete staircase in the west and the timber column in the upper vestibule in red beech deserve special attention. In both materials, concrete and timber, an uninterrupted plastically-formed transition from the bearing support to the load supported is accomplished and the capitals, which, traditionally, were interposed, become plastically overlapping forms. This, too, is an essential achievement of the organically modelled architectural style, as consistently carried out by Rudolf Steiner.

Our building is not intended to cut one off (from the world). Its walls should live. They should live in a way that corresponds to the truth.
Dornach, 28 June 1914

Staircase piers (leading to auditorium)

Spiritual Functionalism

Thus we have now arrived at the question of functionalism. Usually this concept is claimed to describe the architecture of modern objectivity and its origin is attributed to the Viennese Secessionist architect, Adolf Loos. In this case, the concept relates to an architecture stripped of all embellishment, revealing only that which serves a building's functional purpose. However, whereas Loos in reality related form simplification to the purpose (function) of the building in question, his concept was subsequently claimed by the 'Bauhaus' architects for their own quite differently oriented methods.[15] They converted Loosian functionalism into a generalized pattern of Cartesian spatial units, which can be applied for any given purpose ('dividing up the living space'). However, as Janik and Toulmin correctly note, the real functions of the buildings were not revealed, but were in actual fact concealed ('so producing the familiar concrete and glass slabs or shoe boxes to which the name "modern architecture" became attached from the late 1920s on.') If we return to the original idea of functionalism, as it was conceived by Loos, it proves

Lobby to the Great Hall of the first Goetheanum (known as 'Red Beech Room')

to be a further forward-looking ideal of art at the turn of the century, which experienced a climax and continuation in Rudolf Steiner's architecture. Measured against this ideal, his 'structural ornamentation' is not superfluous embellishment but precise artistic expression of a function – only that this function relates to something materially intangible like the 'support' or the 'load', etc., as we saw in the example of the pillars. In this sense, Loos had considered the painter, Kokoschka, a master of ornamentation because he used this to express the inner nature of his subject.[16] Rudolf Steiner's 'structural ornamentation' has *elevated the principle of functionalism based on objective simplification to a functionalism which is spiritually alive.*

The first Goetheanum under construction – 14 March 1914

Topping-out ceremony with the workmen – 1 April 1914

Setting the capitals on the columns

Peace and harmony will flow into the hearts of men through these forms. Such buildings will be lawgivers. The forms of our building will be able to achieve what external institutions can never achieve. My dear friends, however much study may be given to the elimination of crime and wrongdoing from the world, true healing, the turning of evil into good, will in future depend upon whether true art is able to send into human souls and human hearts a spiritual medium. Then, surrounded with full understanding by what has been achieved in architectural sculpture and other forms, these human souls and hearts, if they are inclined towards falsehood, will cease in their untruthfulness; if they are inclined to be disruptive, will cease to disturb the peace of their fellow men. Buildings will begin to speak. They will speak a language of which people have as yet not even an inkling.

Nowadays people gather together in congresses in order to arrange their affairs. They believe that what passes from mouth to ear can actually create peace and harmony. Peace, harmony, conditions worthy of the human being, will only come about when the Gods speak to us. When will the Gods speak to us?

Dornach, 17 June 1914

Top: Column bases – large rotunda

Middle: Wood-carving on the capitals

Bottom: Capital of the fifth column (Mercury Column)

Opposite Page:
Left: the 'Boiler House'

Right top: 'Boiler House' under construction

Right middle: 'Boiler House' – 6 February 1915

Right bottom: 'Boiler House' – 6 February 1915

Model of 'Boiler House' by Rudolf Steiner – 1913

The 'Gesture' of the Goetheanum

If, with this insight, we now turn to the architecture of the Goetheanum as a whole, new light is shed upon what was discussed above concerning the double domed building. The considerable edifice, comprising 66,000 cubic metres, was conceived as an assembly hall for approximately 900 people. In the form of lectures and artistic performances, its visitors are to establish contact with a world of true spiritual experience. – These visitors come from a world where experiences are made mainly through the senses. They search for answers to the questions which life in a material world releases in them but which can only be found in the spiritual world, which they are yet to discover. They seek the reality of this spirit. They strive for inner peace in order to approach the spiritual realm, and wish to go freely and of their own resolve. It is clear that the experience of the interior space of the double cupola, as described above, corresponds with this 'function'. But also its exterior has its own task to fulfil in the functional context: it has to reveal what is happening in the interior. The merging of the cupolas indicates how the world of the senses meets and penetrates the world of the spirit, which is able to furnish the answers to their questions. The suture between the two cupolas indicates the place where the human being can enter the realm of the spirit and which, in the interior, is allied to the speaker's rostrum, as is appropriate functionally. If the listener consciously penetrates beyond the significant words of the speaker, a degree of spiritual experience full of imagery is opened up within him, which finds its home in the pictures on the stage in the rotunda behind the speaker. The cupola in the east reveals its function to the person approaching it from without by being smaller than the cupola of the auditorium. Not because less space is required for the stage, but because the spirit is always more intense, even if the outward form is small. In this way the form of the building voices its function. The task of spiritual fuctionalism is to find for every structure the appropriate, individual form.

The 'Gesture' of Utility Buildings

At this juncture, reference must be made to two utility buildings, which Rudolf Steiner had erected near to the Goetheanum. He designed them himself and chose reinforced concrete as building material for both. The first, the 'Boiler House', arose in 1915, that is, at the same time as the first Goetheanum. It lies to the north-east of the main building, which it heats by means of an underground piping system. Under normal circumstances, something resembling a factory chimney might have been expected to arise here, which in its misconstrued 'functionalism' would have encroached upon the countryside and the adjacent building. The unusual form which it received proceeded, however, from Rudolf Steiner's correct interpretation of its function. Like a threatening mon-

We enter with reverence into the spirit in order that we may become one with the spirit streaming into the forms – for surrounding us are the Spirits of Form; in order that we may become one with the spirit that begins to move – for behind the Spirits of Form stand the Spirits of Movement. This is the *new* architectural thought!
Dornach, 28 June 1914

ster, a sphinx, the building lies in wait on the brink of the hill. Two small cupolas set apart from one another to the fore of the chimney appear like the paws of a strange beast. The chimney itself, growing directly from the body of the building, casts out horn-like growths on both sides. If one witnesses the heating plant in operation and the clouds of smoke issuing and quickly dispersing from its chimney, one begins to understand the language of its form, which expresses the creative forces inherent in heat, steam and smoke. A totally different structural gesture had to be found for a small transformer house, which in 1921 was erected close by the café and restaurant to the south-west. Its forms are rectilinear, the arm-like extensions jerkily thrust forward. The lintel appears to give way in the middle, as if it has received a blow from above. This building served electric commutation processes and its form had thus to manifest something quite different than that of the heating plant, which served the heating processes of coal and water. The forms of these two utility buildings illustrate more clearly than anything else that Rudolf Steiner's spiritual functionalism did not stop at projects to serve cultural purposes, such as theatres, etc., but was capable of encompassing a whole world of technical, utilitarian architecture and of lending it artistic form. Precisely concrete, which is increasingly being applied as a building material, is excellent for this purpose. If our concrete era had adopted Rudolf Steiner's individualising functionalism instead of the down-grading constructivism of the 'Bauhaus', we would still feel ourselves artistically appeased and animated even in an industrial milieu. Imagine if every petrol station, airport or department store were to speak a different architectural language of form! How interesting and how 'human' the world would be! It pertains to the tragedy of our century that the ideal of 'Eloquent Concrete' (Rex Raab), the ideal of individual and eloquent structural forms derived from a precise, spiritual functionalism, has since Rudolf Steiner's age only very rarely been realized and has not been carried through to its last consequence. The commendable efforts of Saarinen (TWA-Building, Kennedy Aiport, New York) and Utzon (Opera House in Sydney) illustrate how difficult it is to arrive at satisfactory solutions. Everything depends upon spiritual functionalism struggling through to achieve an appropriate, individual structural form in every instance. Only then will concrete really begin to speak.

Timber and Concrete

The application of timber and concrete during the initial construction stages on the hill already indicates that all the architectural achievements, which we later encounter in the concrete architecture of the second Goetheanum, had already been accomplished in the first Goetheanum and its adjacent buildings. This is often obscured by modern man's inability to grasp the inner relationship existing between form and

'Transformer House' 1921 – Design by Rudolf Steiner

Between the cupolas of the first Goetheanum

material. The fact that concrete requires rounded surfaces, whereas timber demands a more facetted curvature, gives rise to basic differences in their modelling. At this juncture, it should be pointed out that Rudolf Steiner had not wished to build the first Goetheanum in timber but in a more durable material. The late Dutch publisher, Pieter de Haan, assured me on more than one occasion that Rudolf Steiner had mentioned to him after a meeting concerning the new building project that the members, not he, had proposed a timber construction (members = of the Anthroposophical Society founded in 1913).

Between the cupolas of the first Goetheanum

Right: West wing of the first Goetheanum

North wing of the first Goetheanum

The concrete substructure of the first Goetheanum

Capitals and architraves in the large rotunda. Model by Rudolf Steiner

The Achievements of the New Style

If we follow Rudolf Steiner's steps from the Munich Congress to the erection of the first Goetheanum, we are able to trace the following achievements on his part: By introducing the principle of metamorphosis to construction, the flagging organic style in architecture was restored to its original strength and thus a vital alternative was created in the face of spreading cubism. The reconciliation of all art forms in an integrated work of art, as had been the ideal of Art Nouveau artists, was now realized. The bald functionalism (Loos), which had arisen within the 'Jugendstil' impulse, was heightened to a spiritual functionalism. Thus structuralism which concealed the real functions of an edifice (Bauhaus) was confronted with a functionalism which individualized every detail. The as it were personal structural gesture of every building overcomes the anonymous, levelling stereometry of so-called 'modern architecture'. By introducing interpenetrating cupolas into architecture, a perfect variable equilibrium was for the first time attained in spatial arrangement. Thus the constraints enforced by the stereometrical forms of structuralism were confronted with a liberating element, which permitted the human being to find the motives for his movement within his own being. The real organic living style in architecture is only substantiated if all these elements are present. This style differs from cubism with its *paratactically* assembled structural elements in that the entire building forms one organism. That is, every detail is *hypotactically* coordinated with the whole; totality creates individuality.

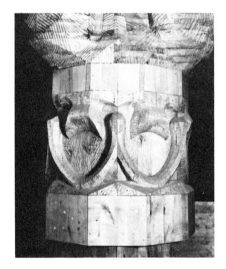

Capital of the sixth column (Jupiter Column) in the large rotunda

This building is intended to be the external representative of the spiritual scientific movement.
Zürich, 28 October 1919

Large rotunda with organ loft

Left: Small rotunda

The Experience of the Interior Space

Before we move on to the second Goetheanum, let us once again step inside the interior of the first building. The effect which its spatial arrangement has on the visitor has already been discussed and represents a decisive feature of this new style in architecture. Rudolf Steiner went as far as to emphasize that in future a work of art can no longer be described by mere reference to its colours, forms, etc. He interprets a true work of art as being first composed in the soul of the person experiencing it. As difficult as this aesthetic problem is to comprehend intellectually, all the more evident will it become to the person capable of perceiving the experiences induced by the interior architecture of the first Goetheanum. The simultaneous experience of rest and movement (cupola and longitudinal axis) makes it possible to pass on freely from an experience of rest to that of movement or from movement to rest, whereby the slightest deviation from the given variable equilibrium causes the compensating counter-force to immediately become active in the experience. Thus, the

If we carry this spatial system of lines and forces, constantly active in us, out into the world, and if we organise matter according to this system, if we detach this system of forces from ourselves and order matter in accordance with it, then architecture arises. All architecture consists in projecting into the space outside ourselves the laws of our own human body.
Dornach, 29 December 1914

Naturally one can criticise in every possible way this architectural style which has been formed out of spiritual science. But nothing that makes its first appearance is perfect, and I can assure you that I know precisely all its flaws and that I would be the first to say: If I had to put up this building a second time, it would be out of the same background and out of the same laws, but in most of its details, and perhaps even totally, it would be different.

Berne, 29 June 1921

soul experiences either restful motion or active rest. It always feels itself to be free and active in the centre of what is taking place. Both are spiritual qualities. This replenishment of the visible form by its corresponding spiritual resonance is made even more obvious if we now consider the experience afforded by the series of metamorphoses on the capitals and column bases. As the columns are erected in two curves accompanying the walls of the rotunda, they do not seem to be pointing out the way like the columns of a basilica, but rather have a static effect — that of holding the onlooker to the spot. The diversity of forms on their capitals and bases at first appears to hinder the eye's passage along them. If, however, the onlooker himself makes the spiritual exertion of inwardly executing the transition from one form to the next, the intervals between the columns will become for him living, moving forms which his soul looks upon and which guide him forwards, where the visible form appeared to hinder his progress. Thus it is clear that the work of art in the row of columns is first accomplished in the onlooker's soul. A prerequisite for this is his spiritual activity, whilst contemplating the work of art. Without this, the work of art is not revealed to him; it remains dumb. This, too, is a feature of true modern art: it summons man's inward participation. He has to be active if he wishes to perceive the work of art at all.

The superimposed sculptural achitraves linking the columns follow the concealed directional movement in the series of metamorphoses. If the onlooker's attention is turned towards them, he notices that they exhibit restrained, recessed forms up the centre column, whereas they then sweep forwards in full plastic relief towards the small cupola. If he allows himself to be influenced by this ebb and flow of forms, his initial experience is that of being drawn into the stream of movement himself, then – in the exertion of curving outwards from within – he feels an individual contribution in creating this current. This experience places him within the evolution of mankind, which first proceeded from the spirit, but was then summoned more and more to actively shape its own destiny.

All the given directional experiences evoked by individual spiritual activity lead up to the figure which found its place at the end of the axis of symmetry in the small cupola: the plastic group of the representative of humanity, struggling for equilibrium between the forces of seductive light and oppressive darkness. It embodies the spiritual counterpart of that which could be experienced in the large cupola as a liberating equilibrium. The human being who is able to interpret the experiences conveyed in the Goetheanum Building feels himself to have been given the freedom which will enable him to begin to act on his own initiative. Humanity's representative has to apply all his cosmic force to establish the human being's necessary state of balance. In this image is perceived the source of the forces which are manifested in the artistic forms of the first Goetheanum.

Rudolf Steiner's first design for the wooden sculpture (1914), executed by Edith Maryon

Left: Rudolf Steiner at work on the wooden sculpture in the carpenters' shop

Left below: Large model of the wooden sculpture – detail of Ahriman

The wooden sculpture

Right: Large model of the wooden sculpture – detail of Lucifer

Below left: Large model of the wooden sculpture – detail of Ahriman

Below right: Profile of the central figure of the wooden sculpture, the Representative of Man

Central figure of the wooden sculpture – the Representative of Man

Carved speaker's rostrum from the 'White Hall' in the first Goetheanum

Above right: The 'White Hall' in the first Goetheanum

Below right: The base of the Saturn Column illuminated by the coloured glass windows – Watercolour by Wilfried Norton

We have indeed reached a time in which, if man's living contact with the world is not to atrophy completely, it is essential that we begin to dive down into the spiritual waves of the natural forces, that is the spiritual forces lying behind nature. We must once more gain the ability not merely to look at colours and apply them here and there as external surfaces but rather to live with them, to experience the inner living force of colours. We cannot achieve this by merely studying the effect of a painting or determining the effect of a colour in this or that spot, that is by merely staring at a colour. We can only achieve it if with our soul we submerge ourselves in the manner in which red, or blue for instance, flows and streams; we can only achieve it if the flowing and streaming of colour becomes directly alive for us.
Dornach, 26 July 1914

Painting in the small cupola in the first Goetheanum – Detail

'Boiler House' and Goetheanum – Watercolour by Hermann Linde

The Goetheanum – Watercolour by Hermann Linde

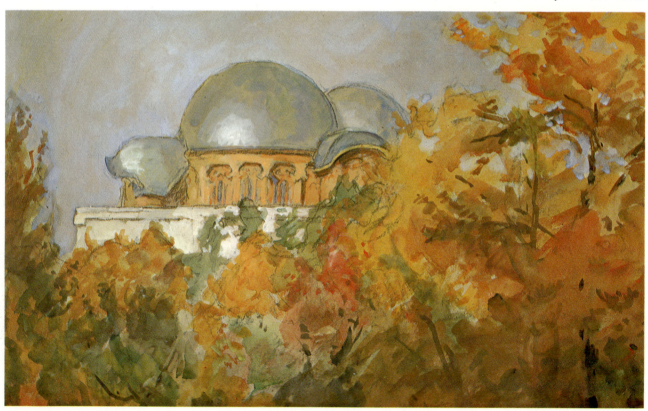

In eurythmy we present in the form and movement of the human organism a direct external proof of man's share in the life of the supersensible world. When people do eurythmy they are linked directly with the supersensible world.

Wherever art is formed from a truly artistic conviction it bears witness to the connection of the human being with the supersensible world.

Dornach, 12 September 1920

Eurythmy group – left to right Emica Senft (Mohr), Friedel Simons (Thomas), Maria Schuster (Jenny)

The first Goetheanum with 'Glass Studio' and carpenters' shop

The 'Carpenters' Shop Hall' with stage 1923

Duldeck House from the south-west

Right below: Duldeck House – roof in the south-west

Opposite: Duldeck House from the north

Duldeck House – south-east entrance

50

The spiritual science of Anthroposophy is no mere theory. It is life itself in all fields and has been able to bring about its own architectural style.
Berne, 29 June 1921

Opposite:
The first Goetheanum – north terrace with Duldeck House

Left: The west wing of the first Goetheanum

Middle: Carpenters during the construction of the first Goetheanum

Below: The first Goetheanum between Arlesheim and the valley of the Birs

The concrete ruin of the first Goetheanum after the fire of 31 December 1922

Right: Blackboard sketch by Rudolf Steiner – Basic motif for the second Goetheanum

Below right: Model (1:100) for the second Goetheanum by Rudolf Steiner – mid-March 1924

You must, however, not forget that this new Goetheanum is to be built with a material which itself is relatively new, namely reinforced concrete. To bring about in a concrete building an appropriate and yet truly artistic style is extremely difficult. A very great deal is needed to solve this problem.
Dornach, 31 December 1923

THE SECOND GOETHEANUM

Hagen Biesantz

On New Year's Eve 1922/23, the first Goetheanum was burnt to the ground. The first total work of art of modern times was destroyed. Would its creative force prove strong enough to confront 'modern architecture' – which was losing itself in Constructivism and Subjective Expressionism – with a new building expressing true equilibrium? This question had to be considered by all those who in the first Goetheanum had witnessed the evolution of a new architectural style. Rudolf Steiner was aware that this creative force was not present in artistic experience alone, but that it had its origins in experiences which were revealed only to the artist seeking access to the spiritual reality obscured by the material world. Modern man's approach to this must proceed from a reflected consciousness, as it is cultivated by the methods of anthroposophical spiritual training. Rudolf Steiner's initial task was therefore to ensure that the Anthroposophical Society, which had been formed to foster spiritual science, received new strength. This was achieved by its refounding as the General Anthroposophical Society at Christmas 1923. With this society, which was conceived as world-wide and independent of national or professional classifications, was incorporated a Free School of Spiritual Science, which commenced its activity in February 1924 and was to establish the methods and contents necessary for the individual's spiritual development. Sections were founded for the various areas of its members' activity. The *Fine Arts Section* – as might appear symptomatic for an organically plastic architectural impulse – was entrusted to the English sculptress, Edith Maryon, who, since 1914, had worked together with Rudolf Steiner on the sculptural 'group' in wood of the representative of man. This sculpture was still incomplete at the time of the fire and was therefore outside the main building in a lofty studio of the so-called carpenter's shop (building hut). Thus it was saved from being destroyed and is today the only work of art in wood (still unfinished) to remain from the old building. Rudolf Steiner's active and direct contribution to the work of this section was already indicated at the Foundation Meeting of the General Anthroposophical Society, when he informed members that he would conduct the Fine Arts Section himself with Edith Maryon's assistance and even voiced his initial ideas on the Goetheanum's reconstruction. Naturally a repetition of the old forms could not be

> It will not be necessary to make the height of the new Goetheanum appreciably greater than that of the old Goetheanum, since I do not intend to have a domed structure again. Instead there will be a facetted roof the flat surfaces of which will harmonise spatially in a way that is no less aesthetically attractive than a domed structure.
> Dornach, 31 December 1923

> Forms in concrete will have to be quite different. A great deal will have to be done on the one hand to master this awkward material properly so that the eye of the human soul can follow its forms artistically. On the other hand it will also be necessary to form artistically by painting or sculpture certain elements which may seem decorative but which in fact arise out of the use of concrete as the building material; thus concrete as a building material can also be revealed artistically.
> I ask you now to treat this germinal thought as the one from which the Goetheanum is really to come forth.
> Dornach, 31 December 1923

> If the Goetheanum is to be built in concrete, it must proceed from an original conception. Thus all building in concrete to date is actually no basis for what has to arise here.
> Dornach, 31 December, 1923

considered, although a metamorphosis of the building conception to accommodate the more intractable material of reinforced concrete would be possible. This time he stipulated the material himself. Indeed, the various remarks Rudolf Steiner made at this time make clear that he himself, and not the members, would now be guiding the project in every detail. We will later see how this fact was also manifested in the structural features of the new building.

As to the design, construction and structural history of the second Goetheanum, an excellent book, entitled *Eloquent Concrete*,[17] has been written by Rex Raab, Arne Klingborg and Åke Fant. A study of this publication, with its extensive illustrative material, is indispensable in forming a pertinent judgement of all aspects of the new building. The following descriptions are largely based on this work.

The Building Conception and Model

Rudolf Steiner first made reference to the new building conception at a meeting of the Anthroposophical Society on 1 January 1924. With the aid of a blackboard sketch, he elucidated the conversion of the main plastic *motif* on the exterior of the first Goetheanum to its appropriate concrete form. It was essential that the elements of support and load were again manifested and that part of a pentagon be described within the centre of the load *motif*. Moreover, more angular forms were now in evidence instead of the rounded forms characteristic of the domed building. A facetted roof replaced the domes. Rudolf Steiner had no doubt that his first task was to create the most appropriate style for this building: 'Nothing has yet been executed in concrete which can provide a basis for what is to arise here.'[18] It is thus a misinterpretation on the part of Wolfgang Pehnt in his *The Architecture of Expressionism*[19] to consider the forms of the small transformer house, constructed in 1921, as signs of a new, more angular stylistic phase.[20] What he considers to be the characteristics of a new stylistic development are in reality the transformer's appropriate structural features (cf. p. 36).

The most urgent task at hand was now to determine the language of forms which the new building was to express and which would prove whether the appropriate forms of a spiritually conceived functionalism would be able to meet a changed situation on the same site. At the beginning of March, Rudolf Steiner found time to work on the building model. As a basis to go on he used a level, polygonal wooden block, which approximately represented the concrete substructure of the first Goetheanum and a plywood board in the form of the ground plan of the original timber construction. Within three days the model of the concrete building, which today crowns the Dornach hill, was fashioned out of red plasticine.

Left: Rudolf Steiner's model for the second Goetheanum from the rear – 1924

Left centre: West façade of the second Goetheanum on the concrete terrace of the first Goetheanum – Sketch by Hermann Ranzenberger – 1924

Below left: West façade of the second Goetheanum with the new terrace designed by Rudolf Steiner – Sketch signed by Rudolf Steiner and Ernst Aisenpreis – November 1924

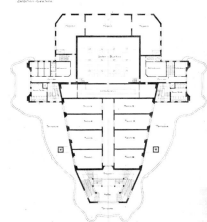

Ground plan of the first storey of the second Goetheanum on the terrace of the first Goetheanum – First building application, 20 May 1924

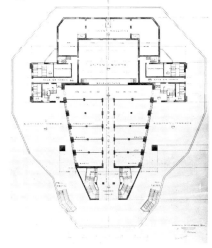

Ground plan of the first storey on the new terrace – Second building application, 11 November 1924

57

Right: Alteration to the stage wing – Sketch by Rudolf Steiner

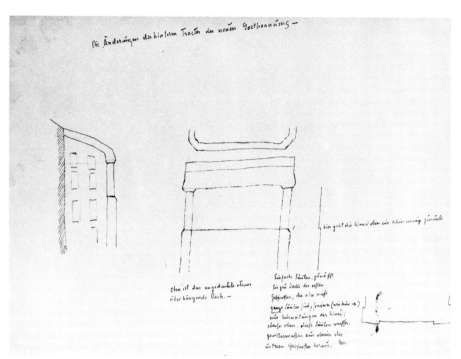

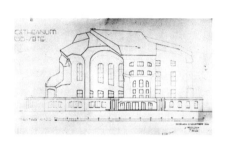

South elevation of the second Goetheanum – Second building application, 11 November 1924

Right: West front – Second building application, 11 November 1924 – Sketch by Hermann Moser

Demolition of terrace of first Goetheanum

Right: West front – Sketch by Hermann Moser

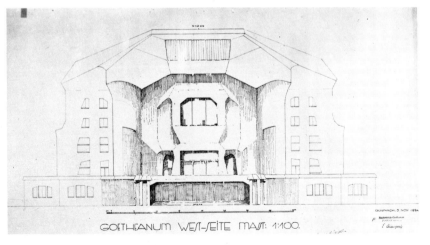

The Architectural Features of the New Goetheanum

The model of the second Goetheanum, which has fortunately survived, must be taken into consideration if the new architectural 'gesture' is to be distinguished in its purity. (Injunctions from the building authorities later gave rise to alterations to the roof and eastern block.) Striking is that the basically cruciform plan of the first Goetheanum has been retained. However, whereas the lateral wings of the first building seem to emerge from the double cupolas and the prevailing impression is that of 'interpenetrating circles', the side wings on the model of the new building together create a clearly defined third element (particularly as a result of the corresponding steps in the roof).[21] The eastern and western sections of the building, that is, stage and auditorium, appear to meet in the refuge of the extended arms of the cross, or to emerge from them. A distinct tripartite division has arisen in the place of duality. Whoever is acquainted with the history of anthroposophical research and relates this with the discoveries concerning the threefold division of the social and human physical organisms, which were not made available to the public until 1917, will immediately understand what Steiner had in mind, when he pointed out that it was impossible to build in 1924 as in 1913.[18]

What is accomplished in the shelter of the middle zone is a new kind of polarity of stage block in the east and entrance front in the west. The former is formed as a plain cubic block (the pilaster-like additions to the corners of the executed building belong to the later alterations), whereas the manifold shapes of the latter are extended towards all those who approach it, as if in welcome. The impression of growing outwards in the west at the same time transforms the polarity into a movement, which takes place from east to west: from the simple rectilinear block, which, like a grain of seed, contains its creative strength hidden within itself, a fulness of organic forms develops towards the west for all to see. It is as if the visitor is visibly witnessing Rudolf Steiner's motto upon the Founding of the General Anthroposophical Society: 'Let that which is formed by the west be fired from the east.' Rex Raab rightly emphasizes that the directional tendency of the sequence of forms in the interior of the first Goetheanum is transferred to the exterior of the second building, but now moving in a reverse direction, that is from east to west.[18] Proceeding from this, as a *motif* of its architectural character, is the fact that the sentiments of the participating members at the time, that is, those who wished as it were to approach the spiritual east from the west, contributed decisively towards the conception of the first Goetheanum, which was developed from its interior space. The new Goetheanum, created from its 'exterior space', had above all to make visible from without that the spiritual forces, which were the source of its creator's experience, sought to be embodied as the organic creative element of western civilisation. This reversal of the directional tendency and the emphasis on 'exterior space' are also related to Rudolf Steiner's own changed position within the Anthroposophical Society. At Christmas 1923 he founded a

This certainly did not mean that an architectural style for a Goetheanum built in concrete existed yet. It will also be necessary in the new Goetheanum to depart in the main from the former concept of a circular building; rather than being round, its forms will tend towards the right angle; it will be a building with angles.
Dornach, 31 December 1923

Now of course, since it will be a matter of having stages for the performance of eurythmy and mystery dramas, the angular building will have to be combined with the round one. In addition the new Goetheanum will need rooms for the various other activities. We shall need studios and we shall need lecture halls, for the single small white hall in which the fire first broke out a year ago certainly proved to be inadequate for our purposes. Thus the next Goetheanum would have to be built with a lower floor, a ground floor and an upper floor. The upper floor would in the main be the large lecture hall, the auditorium for eurythmy, mystery drama and other performances. On the ground floor, beneath this auditorium, divided from each other by walls, would be smaller rooms for artistic and scientific work.

Dornach, 31 December 1923

'Council of Initiative' with the members' consent and himself assumed the chairmanship. (Previously he had only acted as spiritual teacher, without being a member himself.) With this, a new determining factor was added to the hitherto prevailing spiritual needs of the members: the will to influence the cultural circumstances of the western world, 'threatened with decline' (Spengler), creating and healing out of spiritual experience. It would be a misunderstanding to infer from this that Rudolf Steiner would have wished to express such a purpose symbolically in his architecture. He would have declined such an intention as inartistic. For him, artistic forms arose from the immediate experience of spiritual situations, which can be revealed to the historian in the form of ideas, but are conveyed to the artist directly, without any detour by way of thought. Nevertheless, he had himself spoken of a building conception. Yet this rather implied an ideal comprehension of the architectural gesture, which was not bound by any definite conception. Expositions such as those attempted here can never really grasp such gestures and features in their entirety and diversity; they can only rouse the reader's mental alertness to what is characteristic. The architectural gesture has to be seen and experienced; it cannot be thought out.

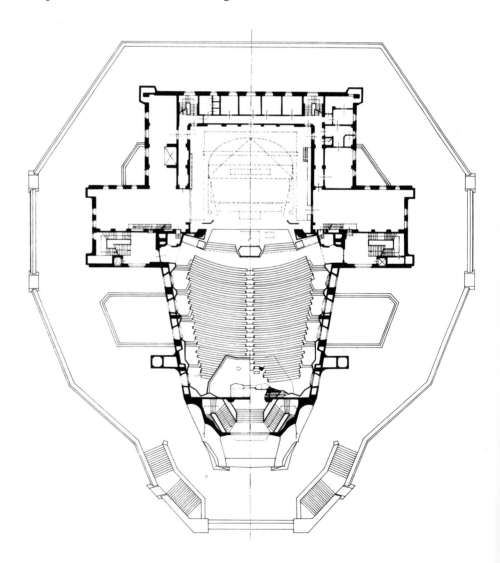

Ground plan at hall level – second Goetheanum

Following two pages:
Top left: Topping-out ceremony of second Goetheanum

Bottom left: Participants in the topping-out ceremony

Right: The Goetheanum freed of its scaffolding – January 1928

The second Goetheanum under construction – 8 April 1926 – Eurythmeum in foreground

Timber form work with steel reinforcement in the western roof area before concreting – 30 September 1926

The second Goetheanum under construction – 10 April 1926

The second Goetheanum under construction – 13 July 1926

The staircase in the west

Right: The staircase in the west – 23 January 1928

Bottom left: The staircase in the south – 16 November 1928

Bottom right: Attic studio in the south – Spring 1927

The Goetheanum from the bank of the Birs – 16 April 1928

Left: The Goetheanum from the south west

Bottom left: The Goetheanum from the west

Where concrete is used one should be able to see in the transitional forms from sloping facetted roof to wall element the expression of downward pressure. I want to achieve also the visual impression that this pressure is caught and held by the portal and window cornices respectively. At the same time I would like to achieve the inward spiritual impression of a portal which receives one or of a window which takes light into the inner space. I also want to achieve with this form in a certain way the revelation of the way in which the Goetheanum is to offer a kind of protection for the person who seeks the spiritual within it.
Dornach, 1 January 1924

Previous two pages:
Top left: The Goetheanum from the north-west with Eurythmeum in the foreground

Bottom left: Partial view from the north-west

Right: Partial view from south-west

The Interior of the New Building

Rudolf Steiner was only able to participate in the initial stages of the second Goetheanum's interior design. On New Year's Eve, 1923, he fundamentally explained the 'building conception' to the members of the Anthroposophical Society.[22] Later, when his illness hindered his presence, he was only able to accompany the work on the building applications by making certain indications. As opposed to the first Goetheanum, the new building was to comprise not only a stage for the Mystery Dramas but also work-rooms for the Sections of the envisaged Free School of Spiritual Science and administrative rooms for the newly founded General Anthroposophical Society. For this reason the building had to receive an additional upper storey and the western staircase be extended to allow enough circulation space for the audience. The upper storey was to admit the stage and large auditorium and the middle storey above the terrace was to accommodate rooms for scientific and artistic work. The ground floor (beneath the terrace) was to contain a stage for rehearsals and other adjoining rooms. This arrangement is essentially that existing today, with the exception that an auditorium for 500 persons (the 'Foundation Stone Hall'), which was not originally envisaged, has been added to the rehearsal stage on the ground floor.

The Great Hall

The Great Hall on the upper storey was first conceived as a rectangle to correspond with the more angular forms of the new building. The stage itself was to be a semi-circle, that is, once again a rounded structure. However, the suggestions which were subsequently made by lighting technicians from the firm of Siemens led to the decision being made to construct a modern technical stage. Accordingly, an approximately square stage with a diorama was envisaged. This situation gave rise to the question of how to reestablish a balance between progression and repose, which had existed in the first Goetheanum. A rectilinear auditorium by its very nature leads the eye in the direction of the stage, compelling the consciousness of the spectator in the same direction. Against this Rudolf Steiner created a compensatory force by transforming the rectangle into a trapezoid, which widens towards the stage. To face the stage is thus more a matter of choice than compulsion. The element of freedom permitted by the double domed building was in this way incorporated in the angular building as well. An orchestra and organ loft were later added to the hall.

The Great Hall admits light through four tall, narrow windows on each side. As in the first Goetheanum, these are of coloured glass in the sequence from west to east of green, blue, violet and pink. After Rudolf

The Great Hall in the Goetheanum

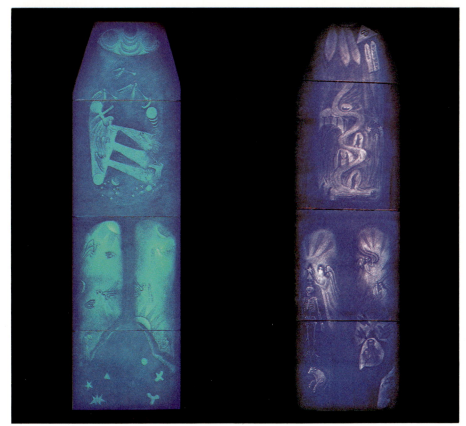

Blue and violet north windows

Steiner's death resort was had to his designs for the glass engravings for the first building.[23] As the new windows did not retain the former triptych arrangement, the themes to either side had to be arranged under the main *motif,* which is not wholly satisfactory from the artistic point of view. Nevertheless, Assia Turgeniev's achievement in incorporating the

69

original window *motifs* in the new building cannot be assessed too highly.

In other respects, the Great Hall remained unfinished until 1957, after a competition had been held and the winning design by Johannes Schöpfer, the Stuttgart architect, was chosen as a basis for its completion. His model did not remain uncontested. A study of the discussions which arose at this time and the alternative models (particularly that by Albert von Baravalle), which were submitted for the competition, illustrates the problems which the architect has to face, if what is inherent in the architecture of the Goetheanum is not only to be preserved but also to be completed artistically. The ceiling paintings, which Rudolf Steiner envisaged and which would have contributed appreciably towards the transparency of the walls as well, have still not been carried out.

The Great Hall (unfinished) – 1928

The Location of the Wooden Sculpture

The statue of the representative of humanity, which had not been damaged by the fire, was originally to have been set up on the new stage. Yet it was soon proposed to accommodate it in a room of its own. Rudolf Steiner is said to have contemplated a wood panelled room.[24] However, a final decision as to its location was not made until after his death. To begin with preparations were made for both eventualities. The eastern stage area was calculated to support the sculpture, which weighs approximately 20 tons, and at the same time plans for a 'Group Hall' were drawn up and sent to the contractor at the end of April, 1925. Finally the separate room at the head of the southern staircase was chosen, which today still accommodates the statue. It was completed in 1935, according to designs by Mieta Pyle-Waller and O. Moser. The walls are not lined with wood, but rendered with a strongly modelled rough plaster. A double wooden staircase leads up to a broad viewing gallery, at which level the models for the first and second buildings have been set up.

Southern Staircase and Ground Floor

The completion of the southern entrance vestibule and staircase was of particular urgency, since the building was entered daily from this side. Carl Kemper, who was also responsible for finalising the model of the western façade of the building, undertook the task of completing the vestibule and its flight of stairs.[25] He developed the forms for the solid balustrade, the walls and their transitions to the ceiling out of the creative

The staircase in the south

principle underlying the building's exterior, the 'living wall'. The hand rail, which was moulded in the same style, incorporated the 'hand movement' principle of the first Goetheanum, corresponding to the profile of a human hand as it takes hold of the rail. The southern staircase and southern vestibule were completed in 1930.

Alterations to the southern vestibule (extension of the entrance hall) were undertaken in 1969-71 by Rex Raab, who tried to maintain as much of Kemper's work as possible. At the same time he planned the 'English Hall' (a lecture hall for English-speaking visitors), opposite the southern entrance. A former storage magazine was extended and converted for this purpose, with seating accommodation for 150 persons and twin projector equipment. In autumn 1971 the room was furnished with coloured murals. Gerard Wagner executed them in plant colours, following the example of the first Goetheanum. Thus, forty-three years after the building was opened, an initial step was at last taken towards realizing what Rudolf Steiner had intended for the interior design of the second Goetheanum: a predominance of colour and painting as opposed to sculpture.[26]

The main room on the ground floor is the 'Foundation Stone Hall', already mentioned, with seating accommodation for 500 persons and a small stage, which has replaced the rehearsal stage originally envisaged. It was planned by Albert von Baravalle in 1952. The very limited financial means available at this time did not permit a more ambitious artistic treatment; an appropriate colour treatment would however much improve the hall.

The 'Foundation Stone Hall', ground level

The Main Staircase in the West

As in the first building, the main entrance is in the west. It leads into a spacious vestibule with staircases on both sides, soaring to the large auditorium above. On the intermediate storey, these stairways open on to a hall-like landing, leading out on to the terrace in the west and into a corridor with rooms for the various Sections in the east. The views from the large front glazed opening and its two flanking windows connect the interior of the building with its surrounding natural scenery. However, if the visitor carries on up the stairway towards the main doors to the large auditorium (second floor level), the large window opposite this entrance does not afford him a similar view of the countryside. It is of red glass engraved with *motifs* designed by Rudolf Steiner, such as the human being encounters when he turns away from nature and looks inwards to contemplate his own spiritual experience.

Left: Cloakrooms on the ground floor

Right: The staircase in the west

The concrete construction of the western staircase with its arches and bracing stands out particularly in the central landing. So as not to obscure the purity of its constructional form, a decision was taken during the completion of the western part of the bulding in 1962-64 to leave this almost in its original state.

The western completion was executed by Rex Raab and Arne Klingborg. They created the doors to the main entrance, designed the spacious cloakrooms on the ground floor, with the adjoining small lecture rooms (Blue and Red Halls), and lent the 'Terrace Hall' (which lies below the terrace to the north) its present form. For the rest, there is a reception desk in the west entrance at ground floor level (south), as well as a booking office, accommodation bureau and book shop (north).

The Exterior Design of the Second Goetheanum

Let us return to the exterior design, which represents Rudolf Steiner's direct contribution to the architectural enterprise. It has already been mentioned that the general disposition of the second Goetheanum was largely determined from outside in, whereas the reverse was the case with the first edifice. Thus, despite all imperfections in the subsequent interior execution, the new style, as it had been conceived by Rudolf Steiner, was nevertheless preserved in its authentic form. It is exhibited in the exterior design of the building as it now stands, and particularly in the original model.

The character and gesture of the design have already been discussed. To this may be added that a completely new type of wall formation in keeping with concrete emerged in the articulated modelling of the western end of the building. Not just the organic 'pulling forth' of ornamental *motifs* from the timber wall, but the plastic movement of the entire wall is here attained. By the convexities and cavities of the concrete (doubly curved surface), a living element, that of inhaling and exhaling, is achieved. In this, the treatment of concrete in the Goetheanum differs appreciably from earlier attempts to mould the concrete wall freely, as, for example, was ingeniously attempted by Antonio Gaudi (Barcelona). Whereas the contour of Gaudi's curvilinear forms shapes the concrete, the contractions and expansions of the Goetheanum's surfaces are experienced as movement of the walls themselves, as breathing life. The contour-like edges only create the border lines (fillets) between the curved surfaces, increasing their inner tension by acting as a boundary. The technical execution of the wall modelling inherent in the model proved to be extremely difficult. We owe it to Ernst Aisenpreis, the architect-in-charge, and to Heinrich Liedvogel, the carpenter, that this task could be mastered. Whereas the concrete dwelling house, 'Haus Duldeck', which was erected on the brow of the hill in 1915-16, had only indicated the initial stages of the new style (in the roof and door construction),[27] the new Goetheanum with its vast dimensions and matured style of surface modelling set far greater demands on those who were involved in its execution. As regards the modelling of the whole, the Goetheanum has remained the only building consistently carried out in this style. Taking into consideration that the principle of the 'living wall' just as much belongs to the fundamental characteristics of the organic building style as that of metamorphosis, it can be estimated how important it was for the future of concrete

Work model for the west façade

architecture that, in the midst of the economic crises of the twenties, the treasurer of the General Anthroposophical Society, Dr. Guenther Wachsmuth, nevertheless succeeded in financing the building from the private resources of the members.

It is far more difficult to discern the metamorphosis principle in the new building than it is to observe the 'living wall'. It has already been mentioned that as early as 1 January 1924, Rudolf Steiner had indicated an open pentagon as the dominant *motif* of the exterior. In an essay in the weekly publication, 'The Goetheanum',[28] Albert von Baravalle has shown how this form *motif* went through several metamorphoses, leading to the western front. It is part of every architect's training to trace this process, advancing from gaining familiarity with doubly curved surfaces to the architectural process of the inversion of building masses, which is a veritable turning inside out. Such exercises are necessary for the further development of an organic architecture, because otherwise a relapse into old, additive forms of construction would be the consequence. An example of such practice is presented in the well-known Pilgrims' Church in Ronchamp (Belfort, 1955) by Le Corbusier, who visited the unfinished Goetheanum building in 1927 and received lasting impressions of it.[29]

The execution of the west front posed a particular problem. An injunction from the authorities to reduce the building's height and the need to widen the lateral wings also appeared to call for a deviation from the model in the entrance front too. Whereas this was achieved without any appreciable aesthetic loss by a proportional reduction of height in the rear of the building, it was feared that the artistic effect of the highly elaborated west front could suffer considerably from the alterations. As the width could not be changed, a reduction in height would have distorted the entire proportions of the carefully balanced modelling. We owe it to the initiative of the sculptor, Carl Kemper, that a solution was

To the true future knower of the spirit, the bridge that can be built between art and seership is more important than any pathological clairvoyance. Those who understand this will know that it will be for the benefit of mankind now and in the future if ever increasingly knowledge of the spirit is sought. The light of seership must shine into art, so that the warmth and greatness of art may fructify the breadth and horizon of seership. This is necessary for art which seeks to penetrate into real existence in the way that is necessary for us if we are to master the great tasks which must approach mankind increasingly from unfathomed depths.
Munich, 6 May 1918

The Goetheanum from the south-west – 14 May 1927

The harmony of support and load is what matters in an angular building. If we now take this over into an organic style of architecture, there will be a revelation in every outward part of its inner nature. For instance the columns, which in the old building reached from the bottom to the top, will have to be transformed in such a way that on the lower floor they develop in a way that resembles roots, architecturally conceived of course. Out of these, the columns proper rise in the region of the upper floor, developing into supports for the whole. From the inside these will then bring the roof, which underneath is not horizontal but encloses the space in the way the dome did, to a completion in its forms. The pillars and columns will be transformed into pilasters and at the same time will express what in the old Goetheanum was to be expressed by the circular structure.
Dornach, 1 January 1924

Top right: Partial view of the south façade

Bottom: Partial views at terrace level

found, which did not diverge from the form of the model: the entire height reduction (of about one fifty-fifth of the height from terrace level, i.e. two feet) was accomplished in the roof.[30] Even if this did imply a less forceful total impression than that conveyed by the model, the purity of the particular (and unique) form of the modelled wall has nevertheless been preserved. In order to co-ordinate Kemper's solution organically with the rest of the building, a further alteration as opposed to the model had to be undertaken: the capital-like terminations of the great lateral piers had to be widened.

The main characteristics of the fenestration, which is often considered unsatisfactory, are traced back to Rudolf Steiner, or arose with his collaboration or consent, as the sketches preceding the building application illustrate.[31] Yet if the present form is compared with the original sketches, alterations are seen to have been made which were not to the advantage of the total impression.[32] A comparison illustrates that the factors disturbing the overall effect were not incorporated until after Rudolf Steiner's death. The window arrangement of the east end[33] was designed by the painter, Henny Geck, also at a later date.

The Overall Impression of the Second Goetheanum

The fortress-like concrete building, which, as Rudolf Steiner himself implied, had been erected for friends and opponents of Anthroposophy alike, makes a peculiarly light and yet dynamic impression, despite its powerful and blocky total form. As Rex Raab has pointed out,[34] this is partly achieved by the fact that the entrance front, also at terrace level, projects westward beyond the respective circles circumscribing the ground plan. An even stronger impression is however gained in this direction by Rudolf Steiner's new interpretation of the function of supports and pilasters. As he demonstrated in his lecture of 1 January 1924,[35] they should have the effect of 'roots become architecture'. Seen artistically, the function of the pillars is therefore not predominantly of a supporting, soaring nature, but above all is experienced as one operating in a downward direction from above, uniting the building with the earth, visibly sinking it into the ground. Thus the supporting element is primarily exeperienced in the broad pillar-heads. These are, however, formed in such a way that they do not merely pass on the pressure of the load downwards, but intercept it to a certain extent themselves, so that sufficient levity or buoyancy remains to manifest the pillars' downward growth. The widening pillar base can therefore be experienced as a rooting element.[36] The essence of organic nature is such that it comprehends not only the plant's upward growth from beneath the earth, but above all its growth from above, which is induced by cosmic forces. It belongs to the tasks of organic architecture to make this evident. The style element of the 'root-like' supports, which seem to grow downwards from above, lends its buoyancy to the heavy concrete building, allowing it to rest lightly, as it were to float above the earth.

West projection from the south

Right: Partial view of the western staircase projection

De Jaager House – model from the north   *De Jaager House – Rudolf Steiner's original model, 1920*

Opposite: *Goetheanum, north side from the west*   Below: *De Jaager House from the north-west, 1930*

*De Jaager House from the south-west –
10 April 1926*

*Wegman House – timber house of the Ita
Wegman Clinic in Arlesheim*

Schuurman House – west side

RUDOLF STEINER'S AESTHETICS

Hagen Biesantz

It is not necessary to have a theory to be able to experience Rudolf Steiner's architecture. Contrary to customary modern art criticism,[37] he considered a theoretical approach to works of art not only as unnecessary but also as misguided. Art should be experienced, not conceived. Nevertheless he placed great value on art appreciation in so far as it was a scientific attempt at understanding artistic creation. Indeed he considered the aesthetics which had arisen since A. G. Baumgarten (1750) as a necessary achievement of modern culture and attributed it to the merits of German philosophy that its representatives strove unceasingly to 'find the most worthy scientific form for the specific manner in which the work of art fuses spirit and nature, ideal and reality'.[38]

Goethe as Founder of a New Aesthetics

To the young Rudolf Steiner it appeared that the premisses of prevailing aesthetics were missing the essential point. In a lecture at the Viennese Goethe Society[38] in 1888, he stated that the initial steps taken by Goethe and Schiller on the subject of the idea of the beautiful ('Idee des Schönen') had been neglected and needed to be taken up again and pursued consistently. He was alluding to Schiller's conception of 'fair appearance' (schöner Schein) and Goethe's perception of archetypes in nature, which together provided the key to understanding art.

At this juncture a modern observer might pose the question whether, in view of the latest developments in art, an aestheticism based on idealism is of any relevance at all. The latter presupposes that a work of art can never be exhausted in the imitation of a natural reality, an interpretation which appears to be refuted by modern surrealism. Rudolf Steiner anticipates this objection by pointing out that nature is always superior to mere imitation since it has reality on its side, whereas art only has appearance. He shares Goethe's conception that a criterion of non-art is an endeavour 'to materialize appearance to such an extent that only common reality remains'. A more fitting definition of surrealism can hardly be conceived.

The task was set of finding out in which sense the reality of art was superior to the work of nature. The starting point was Schiller's argument in his *Briefe über ästhetische Erziehung* (Letters on Aesthetical Education), in which he illustrates that between reason's will to create and natural growth the human being furnishes himself with a space for free play. This 'play urge' is also the root of artistic creativity. What it creates is subject to no restraint. But neither does it have any reality, it is appearance only. The question arises and in the face of modern art becomes increasingly urgent, whether this appearance only reflects the caprice of unconstrained production, or whether an objective reality appears in it in a new way. Rudolf Steiner here leans upon the results of Goethe's studies of nature which indicate how nature in all its aspects falls behind its own intention since every one of its creations is prevented from fully manifesting its own being by the surrounding world implicated with it. It is the artist's task to find 'in the object the point from which something may be developed in its most perfect form'. That is to say, the artist has to recognize the governing tendency in the natural production, its 'intention', and help towards its realization in the material world. 'Artistic creation is not therefore based on what is, but on what could be, not on what is real, but on what is possible.' Thus the artist, who as a human being is himself in the highest sense a work of nature, leads this beyond itself and completes in the work of art the intention of creation. He pays for this liberty by his work at first only having an apparent existence. As this appears in the material world, it nevertheless leads one stage beyond a comprehension of reality which is only ideal. Whereas material experience possesses reality but as yet no intention, which would overcome the incompleteness of this natural reality, science possesses this intention but no longer the reality of nature. Art alone can unite the two. It creates between intention and material reality a third dimension, appearance, within which the human being can participate in the world's creation by revealing a higher reality within reality.

The Essence of the Arts

In the Viennese lecture on 'Goethe as Founder of a New Aesthetics',[38] the 27-year-old philosopher, Rudolf Steiner, formulated his appreciation of artistic beauty and determined a point from which artistic creation can be conceived independently as opposed to science and mere observation of nature. Twenty-one years later, in 1909, he published an unamended new edition of this lecture. As he stated in the preface, the ideas it contained appeared to him to have since become even truer. This paradoxically formulated assertion contrasts with his sentiments at the time relating to an intellectual pursuit of art, which he described in a lecture at Dornach in 1921.[39] As early as 1888 he felt himself 'to be like a mute who can only point at what is essential and which can never really be expressed in philosophical language'. By 1900 this sentiment had intensified and in retrospect he confessed: 'I wanted to express myself whilst still remaining within the artistic experience itself. And I spoke in such a way as carefully to avoid slipping into philosophical formulation.'[39]

This corresponds with the stage in life of the 48-year-old Rudolf Steiner, who had just begun to work as a creative artist himself (cf. Chapter 1, Munich Congress in 1907). He was growing more painfully aware of how 'inartistic the mere concept' was, and how worthless abstract summaries, such as are expressed in the word art, must appear. What he had put in general terms as a scientist proved for the artist a multiplicity, whose different aspects were each subject to their own laws.

The lecture he held in Berlin in 1909 for the members of the Theosophical (later Anthroposophical) Society,[40] was accordingly concerned with the very 'Nature of the *Arts*', whose plurality was now discussed individually. The style of the lecture is purely artistic, seeming rather like a fairy tale. The contents certainly present an abundance of new observations on the relationship between the individual arts and the material and spiritual worlds. No longer are these worlds referred to in general or in the abstract form of a world of ideas, which could be misinterpreted as mere human conceptions. The speaker, who has meanwhile emerged as spiritual investigator, illustrates how the individual arts are each connected with a particular sense organ and how the human senses stand in a precise relationship to different beings of the spirit world. The artist's soul is united with these beings when he is immersed in the sensory sphere of his art. The limits of an art result from the character of the respective being. If it is disregarded, a distortion or caricature of the given art arises.

An example is the art of the dance, which was treated of first in the lecture. In accordance with his doctrine of the twelve senses of man, Rudolf Steiner relates the dance to the sense of equilibrium which has its physical organ in the ear of the human being.[41] The spiritual being manifested in this sense organ belongs to the 'Spirits of Movement' and is able to release the sense of equilibrium from the fetters of the earth. The art of dancing can thus transform repose into a roundelay, which again takes on a definite form as it comes to rest. The Spirit of Movement is brought up to the sphere of the 'Spirits of Form', which can only be approached, never really entered. If the form-element were too strong, the dance would be corrupted. Only in a dance which keeps the form in motion can the harmony of the cosmic planetary movements be contained. The conception of 'Eurythmy' (the new art of movement) is here anticipated, which was later created by Rudolf Steiner and which received its own stage at the first Goetheanum.

It is evident that the limits of philosophical aesthetics are here exceeded to implicate the field of spiritual observation in art appreciation. Henceforth, aesthetic enquiry was directed more and more towards the relationship of art to the spiritual realm.

Impressionism and Expressionism

In the last year of the war, 1918, five years after construction work on the first Goetheanum had commenced, Rudolf Steiner spoke in Munich, the City of the Arts, on *Das Sinnlich-Übersinnliche in seiner Verwirklichung durch die Kunst.**⁴² At that time discussions on the currents in art known as Impressionism and Expressionism were already taking place. Rudolf Steiner saw in the emergence of these concepts a sign that the abstractions of modern art appreciation were growing closer to the reality of contemporary art than had been the case in earlier epochs. He first illustrates this in the relationship existing between the subconsciousness of the human soul and creative impulses. In the depths of every soul exists a sum of experiences which are withdrawn from consciousness. These experiences endeavour 'to break through to consciousness'. They aspire to be transformed into a vision but are unable to do so in a healthy human being, for whom 'this striving towards a vision' has to remain mere aspiration. Vision must not become reality. The impulse, which cannot be realized, can nevertheless be appeased in a healthy manner when the soul is confronted with artistic images from without, which compensate its visionary urge. Imagery which accommodates this need may be termed Expressionistic.

Thus a completely different criterion of art appreciation results for Expressionism than that concerning the relationship between art and nature in *Goethe as Founder of a New Aesthetics*. In the sense of Expressionism thus implied we are able to create a real work of art if our justified visionary aspirations enable us to perceive what form or image we must offer the soul to compensate its visionary strivings.

Impressionism is quite a different matter. Rudolf Steiner's expositions on the subject in 1918 are easily linked with what was generally implied about art in *Goethe as Founder of a New Aesthetics*. The human being looks outwards into nature. He intimates its hidden secrets, which we recognize from Geothe's observations of nature to be the tendencies of natural creation, but which are not fully manifested. Rudolf Steiner now adds that everywhere in nature a lower form of life is subordinated to a higher principle, whereby the tendencies of the lower form of life are unable to develop fully. Every organism is composed of part-organisms, whose individual tendencies are inhibited by the higher tendency of the whole organism. The artist is able to place himself within nature's hidden aspirations and, by lending them form, can thus unveil its secrets.

Rudolf Steiner explains the process in the example of the human form. Two opposing elements are maintained in it and the innate tendencies of each are held back: the head and the remaining organism. If the head were metamorphosed as a whole organism, it would ossify the human being, constrain him, drive him to sclerosis. If on the other hand the remaining organism were given up to its own tendency, the rudimentary growths, which are ossified in the shoulder blades, would develop to wings which would surround the head and join with the extending ears. Both the ossified and the winged form were embodied in Rudolf Steiner's 9½ metre high wooden sculpture (see p. 42 ff.) and confronted with a balanced human form representing the higher life of the whole organism. This sculpture is in this sense an example of Impressionism.

The Munich lecture goes beyond *Goethe as Founder of a New Aesthetics* in two respects. On the one hand it illustrates that the general conception of locating the point 'from which an object can be developed to its most perfect form' must be differentiated by drawing attention to the tendencies of the part-organisms within an organism (object). To the conception of the individual organism's restraint by the interdependence of all organisms is added that of the suppression of the part-organs of an individual organism by the higher life of the latter.

On the other hand the Munich lecture takes up the phenomenon of Expressionism which arose after 1888 and could not be explained by Goethean aesthetics relating to Impressionism. Rudolf Steiner

---

*Difficult to render without paraphrase in English, say – 'The realisation through art of what is both of the world of the senses and the supersensible realm.' Translator's note.

however interprets the soul's processes, which he described as Expressionism and Impressionism, as not only being associated with modern art but also representing the opposite poles at the genesis of all art. Thus his aesthetics also furnish a key to understanding the art of other cultures and epochs, such as had already been the aim of the Expressionists of the 'Blauer Reiter' group in Munich in 1912.[43]

Artistic Imagination and Spiritual Knowledge

Many artists rightly consider customary aesthetics based on the pattern of natural science as being unproductive. A consequence of this is their rejection of every explanation of the artistic creative process. Rudolf Steiner had to come to terms with this problem, since precisely his spiritual research aimed at consciously penetrating the reality of spiritual life. A second lecture which he gave in Munich in 1918[44] presented him with an opportunity of expressing himself on the subject. He first pointed out that both the spiritual observer and the artist have to do with the spiritual world. Their approaches to it nevertheless differ in one essential point. Whilst observing the spiritual world, the spiritual scientist must exclude every sensory perception and also every reminder of such from his own consciousness. On the other hand, the artist must steer his consciousness through the senses towards the external world and unfold his creative inventiveness with the aid of imagination, which then becomes memory. A relationship is nevertheless established between those two totally different methods of approach in that, although the spiritual scientist can totally efface all *natural phenomena* from his consciousness during his spiritual observation, he is however able to retain an important spiritual content 'from a *work of art* once it has been perceived, which he neither can nor wishes to exclude.' However, each art-form conveys its own experience, which in turn creates its own realm of spiritual cognition.

This process becomes intelligible, if it is understood that mental representation and perception are not present in the state of spiritual research and that feeling and volition have to develop inwardly. If they achieve this, 'a lucid, sharply defined spiritual activity is engendered (within them). An activity is germinated within the soul which is similar to thought formation.' However, this is not commonplace, shadowy thought but a new dimension of experiencing reality, whose 'living thought-forms' embrace space in their creative experience and are 'related to nothing so closely . . . as to the forms which the architect thinks and elaborates'. What assumes visible shape in the spatial forms of architecture and sculpture are thought-forms which the spiritual scientist penetrates in order to enter into the spiritual reality beyond the material world. At this juncture, Rudolf Steiner terms this stage of supersensible knowledge objective or *spiritual intellectuality,* which embraces in particular the essence of the arts manifested in space.

A further stage of supersensible knowledge is necessary in order to experience its relationship to music and poetry. 'It lies not only in developing this spiritual intellectuality but also in being as conscious of our own being's presence beyond the body in the spirit's reality as we are of standing in the physical world, standing with our two feet on the ground, taking hold of objects, etc.' We then develop a new heightened feeling, and a volition which is not manifested in the material world. By experiencing oneself in this will activity, new experiences with music and poetry emerge. Rudolf Steiner compares the new incorporeal feeling experienced in music with the image of Aphrodite, as she rises up from the waves. She represents 'the human soul living in the musical element and ascending beyond it, as it perceives its prophetic vision'. On the other hand, poetry is experienced 'as if creatures of the air were to flutter around Aphrodite as she rises up from the sea, approaching her as manifestations of what lives in space . . .' The graphic manner of presentation indicates that the spiritual scientist is now faced with spiritual experiences whose intimacy cannot be grasped by the hard conceptual forms of philosophical aesthetics. These experiences are nevetheless of particular importance in cultivating an aesthetical judgement since they clearly distinguish everything verbose, which is produced merely from human conceit, from real poetry, 'which arises from the true generative laws of natural creation'.

In this context a particular role is assumed by painting. Its artistic inventiveness transforms everything that lives in space to appear on the surface as line, form and colour. Thus something confronts the spiritual scientist from without, which he himself produces from within, when he wishes to demonstrate inwardly his formlessly experienced spiritual knowledge, that is, when he forms an *imaginative conception*. Painter and spiritual scientist thus create from opposing aspects that which is encountered in human consciousness as image from without and as imagination from within.

If we are to consider the level of consciousness devoid of abstract conceptions, where spiritual science encounters the essence of the arts, the fear can be overcome that this research might encroach upon artistic creativity. The basic factor underlying creative imagination remains in fact in the artist's subconscious. Where it enters the consciousness of the spiritual scientist it is not affected by the 'inartistic mere concept', which has to be overcome from the outset. Thus both conditions of the soul – the artistic and that which consciously indwells the spirit – can exist side by side in the same human being, without imposing upon each other, On the contrary, spiritual science enables a heightened encounter with the essence of the arts, opening up new sources of artistic imagination. Thus at the end of his lecture, Rudolf Steiner quotes a sentence of his pupil, Christian Morgenstern[45]: 'The individual who prefers to immerse his feelings in today's experience of the Divine Spirit rather than to discern its essence is like the illiterate who sleeps every night with a primer under his pillow.'

The Spiritual Origin of Art

Every step taken by Rudolf Steiner to present the supersensible element in art from new points of view has its origin in his axiom of 1888 that 'a work of art is only justified if it in some way transcends nature'. With this statement he also introduces an attempt to break through the boundaries restricting art appreciation to the *artist's experience between birth and death*. At the Free School of Spiritual Science (Goetheanum) in Dornach he presented in 1920 the results of his research in this field.[46] These again pointed towards a differentiation of the arts, this time however from the aspect of birth and death, waking and sleep. He presumed that the members of his audience were all already acquainted with the fundamental principles of anthroposophical Spiritual Science, as now not only the spiritual scientist's or artist's immediate states of consciousness were to be discussed but also the human spirit's forms of existence before birth, after death and during sleep. If this knowledge were not to be considered, a further field of artistic reality would be excluded from art appreciation.

Rudolf Steiner proceeds from the fact that the external form of a work of sculpture or architecture is experienced rather as inner reality. The support and load motifs of constructional elements, the concavities and protuberances of plastic forms are experienced inwardly. Although poetry arises within the human being, it is experienced more externally, particularly if the words are arranged in metres and rhymes, when it is almost as if one had to walk in step with them. 'They populate the atmosphere surrounding the individual more than his inner being.' The same applies to musical notes, which animate his surroundings.

Such aesthetic sentiments, which are only possible in relationship to art and not nature, should not be systematised in a pedantic manner. They should lead to an awareness of the soul's nuances, which are associated with how individual modes of art are experienced. For example, if we inwardly experience the dynamics and mechanics of a building and follow the curves of a plastic form, the inner world of sensibility takes a course similar to the process of memory. This form of memory is superior to the usual form occasioned by natural perceptions. It approaches a spiritual experience, which the spiritual scientist recognizes as a reminder of the prenatal states of the human spirit. How the soul liberated from a former life on earth moves in spirit and together with other beings also experiences direction and equilibrium, is subconsciously registered and reproduced in architectural and sculptural works. 'The fact that humanity has produced architecture and sculpture in its cultural development is basically traced back to the after-effects of life between death and birth.' From this results an inward urge to expose prenatal experiences. With the same necessity as the 'spider spins', the human being feels the impulse to create architecture and sculpture.

Poetry is a different matter. Its prose content refers to things and incidents in our normal life between birth and death. By including rhythms, assonances, rhymes, etc., something is added to the prose content which is not present in everyday life – a stronger psychic force than is required for ordinary life. 'It is a foresight of the life to follow death. Because the individual already bears within him that which is to follow death, he feels the urge not just to converse but to converse poetically.' Similarly we have created music because our soul's organization already sustains its postmortem experience. Here it is a case of growing accustomed to that world's harmony which is traditionally termed the Music of the Spheres.

A third state of human spiritual existence is connected with painting. It is experienced every night in the realm of sleep, when the essence of colour is unconsciously imbibed. If the artist's conscious imagination strives towards a harmony of colour, he allows a supersensible element experienced in sleep to flow into his waking sensory activity.

Painting can also be understood as a manifestation of the spiritual world pervading us, in which we abide in our sleep. Sculpture and architecture are witnesses of a spiritual world to which we belonged before our birth. Music and poetry point towards the spiritual realm which we will enter after death. At this juncture, Rudolf Steiner denotes Eurythmy, the art of movement which he had himself created, as art embracing both prenatal and postmortem experience.

The explanation of the relationships existing between the individual arts and prenatal and postmortem human existence was a significant extension of Rudolf Steiner's spiritual aesthetics. The human being's urge towards artistic activity and the differentiation of the arts proceeding from him can now be understood from his spiritual participation in past and future.

Psychology of the Arts

As Rudolf Steiner extended the field of his art appreciation, he felt himself to be confronted even more strongly with the methodical problems of this research. Thus he commences a lecture on *The Psychology of the Arts* (1921)[47] with a retrospect of the previous course of his investigations and distinguishes three phases. The first two are characterized by his lecture in Vienna in 1888 and by his explanation of the nature of the arts in Berlin in 1909 (cf. page 83 f.). In these, the philosopher's abstract method of elucidation is confronted with the artist's imaginative presentation of spiritual experience. Since 1909, Rudolf Steiner had been struggling for a third interpretation of art, which he terms psychological. His research on the supersensible nature of art, as illustrated in the above paragraphs, results from this effort. In 1921, it receives a new note in so far as it no longer proceeds from the various art genres and their spiritual backgrounds but from the artist's individual forms revealing the essence of his art. Rudolf Steiner no longer wished his observation to be directed towards categorization, but rather towards life itself. 'I was looking for a subject allowing the admittance of life to art appreciation.' This subject was provided in the first instance by his study of the life and works of Novalis.

He found Novalis' poetry expressed the works of a human being whose whole existence was directed towards the spiritual world, whose inmost soul was filled with its harmonies and did not really penetrate the material world. Rather did it touch upon it, whereupon poetic imagination was developed from a musical element resounding with the soul's spiritual experience. On the other hand, Goethe's soul is directed entirely towards the apprehension of that spiritual element which seeks manifestation in the material world. What results, when the surface of things is penetrated and artistic form given to that which is perceived there, is decisive for Goethe's poetry, which is thus related to the spatial arts, particularly to sculpture. In Goethe and Novalis is manifested the polarity of two souls. One is so strong that it penetrates beyond the limits of human sensory organization, the other so delicate that its 'soulful spirituality' stops as it were at the boundary of its own senses. The former, also in his main inclinations, turns rather towards the fine arts, the latter to music. It is easy to see that a further basis for a deeper understanding of Impressionism and Expressionism is presented here (comp. p. 85).

Rudolf Steiner's Aesthetics

Rudolf Steiner's works do not include aesthetics in the sense of a systematical presentation. Such would also be inconceivable in view of his relationship to art. His contribution to aesthetics exists in an abundance of insights, which he wrestles from the aesthetic problems encountered on his life's journey, but which are nevertheless supported by the basic philosophical theory he had presented in his Viennese lecture in 1888. A summary of his later observations would also have to consider the paths that had led him beyond philosophical aesthetics, in the manner described above. Thus his aesthetics could never be explained methodically and would also have to reject the common ideal of completeness.

The fragmentary nature of Steiner's art appreciation (fragmentary in the sense of Novalis) is precisely that which enables the creative artist to gain immediate access to it. He does not feel himself to be laced into the Spanish boots of a conceptual system and is able to experience at first hand how Rudolf Steiner discerns one problem and proceeds to the next, just as the artist makes his way from one work of art to another. Nothing is hard and fast. The eyes are rather opened to something concealed behind the artist's problems in life. It might be said that Rudolf Steiner's aesthetic fragments represent most eminently the aesthetics of the creative artist.[48]

Western front

RUDOLF STEINER'S ARCHITECTURAL IMPULSE IN MODERN ARCHITECTURAL HISTORY

Åke Fant

Rudolf Steiner was already an established philosophical writer when he commenced work on the Goetheanum building. In the 1880's he associated himself with the Romantic tradition and with Goethe, a fact which must not be treated as coincidence but rather has to be understood in its full historical significance.

Rudolf Steiner discovered that Goethe's quest for a fitting modern approach to aesthetics had led him to a completely new mode of nature study and further to the search for conformity to law in the organic world forming the basis of his doctrine of metamorphosis. Steiner's contribution in this instance was to take up Goethe's doctrine of metamorphosis and in his lectures repeatedly demonstrate it to his contemporaries. He had recognized the possibility it presented of throwing a bridge between an intuitively artistic and a scientific mode of observation. He represented the view that artistic sensibility and scientific method could be united in the study of nature, an insight which emerges for the first time in history and which enables a synthesis of the worlds of art and science, which till then had always existed separately.

The true significance of his theory stands out even more clearly if the artistic endeavours at the turn of the century are taken into consideration. After the succession and confusion of the most diverse stylistic movements in the course of the 19th century, the 'Jugendstil' artists had finally attempted to set out upon new ways in architecture and the applied arts. Particularly nature was believed to contain the solution to new problems of style. The strongest impulses in this direction proceeded originally from the Anglo-Saxon world but were soon to become common property of the west.

In the U.S.A., Louis Sullivan was constructing large buildings for commercial purposes whose designs were allied to the laws of nature. Sullivan lent the skyscraper an artistically valid form by comparing its architectural construction with the tree's law of growth. His much quoted dictum 'form follows function' is also based on his observations of nature and was later to be continued in the architecture of his pupil, Frank Lloyd Wright.

In Spain, the architect Antonio Gaudi created architectural forms which also complied with natural laws. Their language of form is so illusionary that the observer is often unable to determine where natural form ceases and architecture commences.

At this juncture, further architects can be listed whose works were similarly inspired by nature: Hector Guimard, Henry van de Velde, August Endell, Victor Horta, Charles Rennie Mackintosh, Joseph Maria Olbrich and many others.

Indeed, a whole generation of architects for a time devoted themselves to the artistic aims of Nouveau Art and to working with natural forms.

This style was however soon to degenerate and new ways were attempted. The leading architects were probably not responsible for this development, but rather their followers. Their artistic work disregarded any functional purpose, with the result that the language of forms, claiming undue independence, became an end in itself. The aspiration which was manifested in the 'Jugendstil' was to create a uniform milieu.

At this time, many painters extended their fields

Antonio Gaudi, Colonia Güell, Barcelona, Spain – 1915

of activity in design and craftsmanship to include architecture. Significant representatives of this development were Henry van de Velde and Peter Behrens.

Many painters were meanwhile endeavouring to proceed from image to true representation. They aspired to depict what they termed a new spiritual reality and renounced the material world for the sake of abstraction. The most significant artist of this phase was Wassily Kandinsky, whose book *Über das Geistige in der Kunst* (Concerning the Spiritual in Art) was widely read amongst artists and intellectuals. In this book, Kandinsky examines scientific and artistic phenomena over several decades, indicating the preparation for a new spiritual era. These phenomena provided him with access to various occult movements consistent with what was at that time taking place. Recent research has shown that Kandinsky was above all influenced by theosophical and anthroposophical circles during his work on the book. It has further been proved that he not only attended Rudolf Steiner's lectures but also studied his essays in the periodical *Lucifer Gnosis*. However, it was not so much Rudolf Steiner's specifically artistic intentions which influenced Kandinsky but rather his interpretation of the present state of humanity.

Up to this time, around 1910, Rudolf Steiner's activities were chiefly theoretically oriented; he wrote books and gave lectures. However, he gradually felt this activity to be inadequate; he wanted to extend the scope of his work. Rooms were then provided for anthroposophical activities and interest kindled in their artistic arrangement. An atmosphere of colour was first created by painting the walls with a glazing technique. The concept of luminous, transparent colour is usually thought to have emerged in painting after the First World War when, amongst others, the German architect, Bruno Taut, strove for colour applied to exterior and interior spaces. Above all he advocated transparent plant colour which, as he writes, reflects cosmic play in nature. He believed that such efforts could only be achieved with the aid of the 'Goethean or Cosmic Doctrine of Colour'. Bruno Taut's interpretation of the Goethean doctrine corresponds exactly with that upheld by Rudolf Steiner before the war. The conclusion that Bruno Taut had received these ideas from Rudolf Steiner himself or through others therefore appears very obvious.

Rudolf Steiner's directions on interior wall painting were soon to be elaborated to comprise a new architectural style. Increasing anthroposophical duties together with the need for a Mystery Drama stage occasioned him to draw up building plans for Munich and then Dornach. In Dornach these plans matured and gradually found their realization. Here,

Peter Behrens, turbine factory, Berlin, Germany – 1909

Rudolf Steiner was able to confront contemporary architectural tendencies in his own manner.

With regard to architecture prior to the First World War, it was evident how strongly national movements were being asserted. Industry went through a period of expansion which decisively influ-

Max Berg, Centenary Hall, Breslau, Germany (now Poland) – 1913

Walter Gropius and Adolf Meyer, Fagus Works, Alfeld/Leine, Germany – 1913

enced architecture. Anonymous industrial buildings in the U.S.A. indicated the direction which European architects were to take and it was studied how various functions could influence architecture. However, this process was not wholly rational. Rather could a trace of Romanticism be discerned in the various architectural forms of expression. The German 'Werkbund' (Confederation of Designers and Craftsmen or Industrial Union) and its consequences also influenced contemporary architecture considerably. Peter Behrens' inclination towards classicism was manifested in his industrial halls for Siemens AEG in Berlin and paved the way for his pupil, Walter Gropius, when he constructed his factory in Alfeld/Leine (Fagus Works). In the remarkably 'modern' design of this factory and its successors, which were displayed at the 'Werkbund' Exhibition in Cologne in 1914, it is noticeable how strong the urge then was to study various materials, for example, glass, from a purely aesthetic point of view. The possibilities of reinforced concrete were also examined from every aspect. In France, Auguste Perret achieved impressive results with this new material and in Breslau, Germany, Max Berg constructed his Centenary Hall in reinforced concrete, attaining a quite incredible cupola span. For the Industrial Union's Exhibition in Cologne, Bruno Taut erected a 'glass house' on a concrete base with braced steel wall construction – the infilling was of glass bricks – and a domed glass roof. This 'glass house' arose in closest collaboration with the

Bruno Taut, Glass House, 'Werkbund' Exhibition, Cologne, Germany – 1914

architect and poet, Paul Scheerbart, a rising architect who advocated an uncompromising glass architecture. On the one hand he saw eternity symbolized in this new material, on the other hand it was to serve as a means of creating a new morality. These three materials, concrete, steel and glass, were thus to form the prerequisites for a new architecture. Then the First World War was declared!

Ever since 1913 Rudolf Steiner had been working on the planning of the site which had been placed at his disposal in Dornach. An international group of artists, architects and amateurs was to help to carry out the 'Johannes Building' project under Rudolf Steiner's own direction. The main construction was designed throughout in timber clad in American oak resting on a concrete substructure. At the same time a series of smaller buildings were under construction on the same site. Entirely in concrete is the 'Boiler House', completed in 1915, with its small twin cupolas and towering chimney branching out in pointed forms. Nearby stands the 'Glass Studio' with its shingle roof and slate covered cupolas. This was completed in 1914. Also constructed in reinforced concrete is the dwelling 'House Duldeck' or 'House Grosheintz'. Its rectangular core is flanked by projecting semi-cylindrical parts with a domical roof treatment.

All these buildings were commenced shortly before the outbreak of the First World War. A colony of surrounding buildings was also foreseen, which was to comprise houses similar in construction to those already envisaged. However, after the war this plan was not realized. The intention had originally been to construct a more extensive spiritual centre with neighbouring dwellings responding to the main building in a similar language of forms. Throughout the entire site the ideas Rudolf Steiner had developed earlier were put into artistic practice. Despite their different functions and execution, the common characteristics of the buildings are nevertheless in evidence even in the available pictures. For example, the distinct modelling of the various cupolas illustrates an important theme which is continued throughout the complex. Although Rudolf Steiner was certainly at pains to develop the principle of metamorphosis further, to embrace artistic form, it was not his intention to transfer a natural form in one way or another to the field of architecture, as had been the aim of the 'Jugendstil' architects, but rather to convey the transformations of living form in architecture. The practical implication of this may be traced from building to building on the site. If the main building is considered by itself, a similar transformation of a formal *motif* is evident, carried out to the smallest detail. This infers that Rudolf Steiner, although advocating a metamorphosis which was true to nature, did not wish to comprise any specific natural form in his architecture. He rather admitted the principles of metamorphosis and translated them freely in his architectural forms. Thus he was able to give a new stimulus to the architectural language of forms which ultimately led to an artistic freedom allowing solutions to architectural problems which were at the same time in accordance with nature.

The question of nature as model for an architectural language of forms had by no means disappeared with the 'Jugendstil' from architectural debate and will be discussed later.

During the war, Rudolf Steiner and his international group of students continued to work in Dornach towards the completion of the main building. Although the work was carried out under the shadow of the war, all participants felt themselves to be working on a work of peace.

 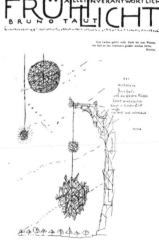

Lyonel Feininger, woodcut 'The Cathedral of the Future', in the 'Bauhaus' manifesto by Walter Gropius – 1919

Title page of the periodical 'Frühlicht' by Bruno Taut, Design by Carl Krayl – 1920

Wassily Luckhardt, 'City Crown' published in the periodical 'Frühlicht' by Bruno Taut – 1920

The First World War brought upheavals to the most various fields of modern culture, including architectural development. In Germany shortly after the revolution radical artists and architects founded the 'Work Council for Art'. Amongst the architects, Walter Gropius and Bruno Taut emerged as leading personalities of a new architecture. No longer being able to associate themselves with the old, pre-war ideals of the 'Werkbund', they aimed to build up something radically new. They had learnt to hate war and had experienced how large cities were no longer in a position to support their populations. Bruno Taut thus propagated a complete dissolution of large towns and cities. In their place, he proposed small settlements in the country where the inhabitants would be presented with the possibility of cultivating enough land to be able to support themselves. At the centre of these colonies a 'Cathedral of the Future', 'Crown of the City' or 'People's House' was to be erected. The inhabitants themselves would be in favour of these buildings and would build them as a common task. Bruno Taut felt that it was the architect's duty to design such buildings which would be dedicated to a new spirituality. As there was practically no money available for new building projects immediately after the war, he felt the time must be spent in preparation for future construction tasks. A group of younger architects supported Bruno Taut's new ideas and drew up plans for such building projects. These ideas were presented in the periodical *Frühlicht* ('Morning Light') and in letter form, 'Die gläserne Kette' ('The Glass Chain'). The concept of a community centre or 'People's Building' was not a specifically German concern in the years after the war. In Holland, Berlage appealed for necessary planning in this direction and published *The Pantheon of the Human Race.* H. P. Berlage's pantheon was also to be a temple of peace standing in the centre of Europe. Like its historical forerunner, it was to be a domed building with 'top lighting'. In the interior, a monument depicting the 'Brotherhood of Man' was to be erected. Bruno Taut and his colleages were meanwhile working on a large glass construction whose forms were inspired by the celestial sphere. The circle around Bruno Taut was stimulated by the poet Paul Scheerbart, who, as already mentioned, felt that glass construction would decisively influence future architecture. In glass architecture he saw possibilities of positively changing morality. Indeed, this moral aspect was of utmost importance for the concept of a 'Cathedral of the Future'. Particularly Bruno Taut and his followers represented the view that modern architecture had to fulfill a moral mission and thus they endeavoured to include moral qualities in their architecture. This was mainly accomplished by creating rooms associated with particular purposes in which one could mutually meditate the world's significance, the meaning of life and death and problems of 'Weltanschauung'. These ideas were certainly relevant for a generation which had experienced the disintegration of most traditional values in the course of the First World War and the time immediately afterwards and now longed for new ones in their place. Bruno Taut and others anticipated a new spirituality which would gradually be apprehended by humanity. As well as they could, they sought to create the prerequisites for this new world in their buildings or at least in building projects which were to serve the new spirit as places of worship. They were convinced that the new spirit would crystallize out of humanity itself and that man, as if following an inner urge, would participate in the construction of these 'Cathedrals of the Future'. These ideas did not appear to be related to any political party but were expressed frequently amongst artists and intellectuals who all longed for a uniform principle upon which life could be based.

The formulation of a universal concept of peace and the foundation of a spiritual centre were also the tasks which occupied Rudolf Steiner prior to, during and after the war. He too strove for a moral consequence in architecture and accordingly investigated architectural forms. Yet he did not wish to attain a moral effect by any particular designation of rooms; the formative strength which had created the wood carvings and paintings was itself to be raised up to the moral sphere. The edifice, the Goetheanum, was itself to give utterance and was therefore a 'House of Speech'. It is not clear to what extent Steiner's contemporaries were aware of his activities in Dornach. It can only be confirmed that in a certain respect similar endeavours are observed amongst architects of this generation and that Rudolf Steiner

Erich Mendelsohn, Einstein Tower, Potsdam, Germany – 1921

Hans Poelzig, Grand Theatre, Berlin, Germany – 1919

totality inspired by nature, which in this case was realized in the form of a huge built grotto. Light sources were concealed behind rows of stalactite-like formations hanging from the theatre's ceiling.

At this time, Erich Mendelsohn constructed his so-called 'Einstein Tower', which was one of the few began at a very early date to convert his ideas into architectural practice.

Another theme which was then topical in Germany, particularly in Berlin, was the discussion concerning art's relationship to nature. Here it may first be noted that the relationship to nature as manifested in Art Nouveau was no longer of interest, indeed was even opposed. Thus the 'Grosses Schauspielhaus' ('Grand Theatre') or 'Friedrichspalast' ('Friedrich Palace') in Berlin by Hans Poelzig was considered exemplary as representing a whole universe. Modern architecture was to exhibit an organic

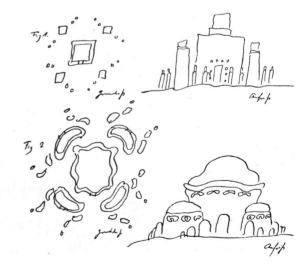

Paul Gösch, 'Mineral and Organic Architecture'. From the periodical 'Frühlicht' by Bruno Taut – 1920

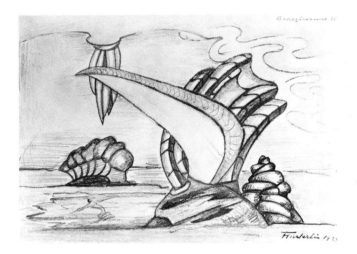

Hermann Finsterlin, 'Bathroom' (sketch) – 1925

Gerrit T. Rietveld, Schröder House, Utrecht, Holland – 1924

projects to be realized in this architectural period and which is unique in its organic totality. Clearly he received his inspiration for this building from the form world of sand dunes piled up by the wind and for the surface treatment from the symmetrical structure of bones.

Similar endeavours were manifested amongst Bruno Taut and his friends. As they were unable to realize any of their designs, their relationship to nature can only be inferred from their sketches and utterances. Bruno Taut strove for a cosmic architecture in which a multitude of star and crystal glass forms were to be translated into buildings. Bruno Taut's friend, Hermann Finsterlin, sought to continue God's creation where it had ceased on the seventh day. His projects were attempts to establish a continuity between landscape, garden, house and furniture which would give rise to an all-embracing unity. A further architect in Bruno Taut's circle, Paul Gösch, created in his architectural visions a structural world which proved to be inspired by theosophical conceptions: architecture closely related to nature. All these architects believed that an architecture at one with nature would be imbued with the new spirituality which was to emerge. This is articulated in particular in Walter Gropius' remarks at this time when he was developing his initial concepts for the 'Bauhaus'. All had faith in the 'Cathedral of the Future' which was to be erected with the support of many thousands of craftsmen.

At the beginning of the 1920's a considerable group of German architects thus endeavoured to construct a completely new philosophy of life, a new consciousness in which concepts such as spirit and a close association with nature live in a strange symbiosis which we have difficulty in understanding today.

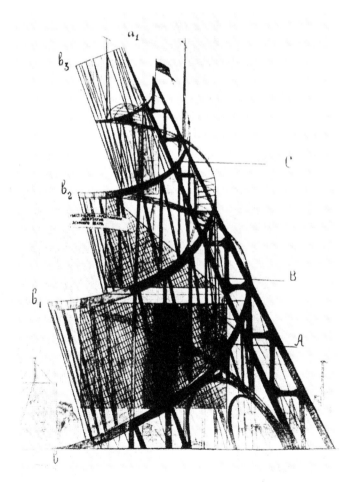

Wladimir Tatlin, project for a monument for the third Internationale – 1919 to 1920

Le Corbusier, Studio Ozenfant, Paris, France – 1922

Rudolf Steiner stood in the midst of these discussions concerning nature and spirit; he too strove for the union of both poles. This synthesis was to take place in the first and later in the second Goetheanum building. Rudolf Steiner saw nature as a source of inspiration arousing the developed human spirit to attain a total synthesis with the aid of a third factor, activity. Friedrich Schiller's thesis in his *Briefe über die ästhetische Erziehung des Menschen* ('Letters on the Aesthetic Education of Mankind') can be seen as a prelude to Rudolf Steiner's efforts in this direction. Here Schiller discusses the material urge and the urge to form and finds that the creative person's artistically accentuated play urge is capable of lending shape to the given elements. Similarly, Goethe points out that when man begins to unveil nature's open secrets he is deeply stirred by an irresistible longing for its most noble form of expression, art. Rudolf Steiner's further development of Goethean concepts finally induced him to give the building in Dornach the name 'Goetheanum'.

In other European countries at this time the fundamental attitude was a different one. In Holland, a group of artists and architects founded 'De Stijl' and drew up a manifesto advocating universalism in lieu of the individualism which had been responsible for all that had come to pass in the war. Moreover, they believed that chaotic nature would necessarily have to be overcome by human and superhuman spirit, order thus being brought to disorder. Religion was to be replaced by philosophy.

In Russia, constructivism was developed after the revolution. Here a subjective attitude to things tended to be replaced by a more material, structural approach.

In France, Le Corbusier published his conception of future architecture in the periodical 'L'Esprit Nouveau'. He advocated a completely new spirituality which was also to comprise rational ideas.

All these ideas gradually found their architectural expression in the Weissenhof Housing Estate in Stuttgart (Exhibition 1927) and lead moreover to the development of the concept of 'International Style'.

THE GOETHEANUM IN PROFESSIONAL LITERATURE

Rex Raab

Whereas many a striking building of our century is reflected in the mirror of literary publications as an annual plant which blossoms quickly and magnificently but just as rapidly withers and sinks into oblivion, the Goetheanum appears rather as a hardy perennial which, to the surprise of the bystanders, continues to bloom and to bear many seeds. A shrub often has to take root for a considerable time before manifesting the profusion of its potentialities. Thus the Goetheanum only gradually acquired its reputation and fame in the course of this century. It took root in relative obscurity, despite the fine publications of the Philosophisch-Anthroposophischer Verlag, in a process which continued over thirty years – to be precise, from its inauguration at Michaelmas 1928 to the summer and autumn of 1960. Public discussion was then initiated with great discernment by Willy Rotzler, who was at that time the Director of the Museum of Modern Art in Zurich. In his contribution to the professional journal *Werk*[49] he treats of 'The Goetheanum as an Example of the Integration of the Arts' and indicates from his unprejudiced standpoint that such a result, which must certainly be unique in our age, can only be achieved on the basis of a shared conception of life which is directed towards an appropriate aim. Numerous publications on this reinforced concrete building followed.

It cannot be otherwise with a work resting on a profound spiritual foundation, although the media are misleading. A third of a century is not long if in this time people have become aware of the existence of an artistic landmark and a living building impulse has begun to bear fruit.

This process is clearly traced in *Eloquent Concrete*[17] (1972), which is primarily devoted to the second Goetheanum. It was a complex process representing a critical discussion, largely on the part of the professional world, of what Rudolf Steiner had called into being and others have taken up. Furthermore it illustrates various attitudes and tendencies which are subject to constant change. In this case we will restrict ourselves to the diverse response in the professional press which has been evoked by Rudolf Steiner's architectural enterprise, in particular the concrete construction of his second Goetheanum. Recent publications of the Verlag Freies Geistesleben, Stuttgart, *Der Bau* by Carl Kemper and *Rudolf Steiner als Architekt von Wohn- und Zweckbauten* by Erich Zimmer[50] have already been reviewed elsewhere. However, if the reader is to form a correct picture, he must always be aware of the particular circumstances of a given period.

In 1928, when the second Goetheanum – still unfinished – was inaugurated, amazement was voiced in the international press at the Anthroposophical Society's achievement which, in the immediate wake of Rudolf Steiner's own activity, was seen to be something prophetic. Thus, Kenji Imai,[51] the Japanese architect and author, who two years earlier, in 1926, had gained first hand impressions of progressive architectural movements in Europe, including Dornach, felt it to be his moral duty to report in his native country on the opening of the Goetheanum, which, at the time of his visit, had been largely concealed by scaffolding but had nevertheless stimulated his interest. He drew attention to the cultural tasks based on a study of Goethe which were undertaken by the Free School of Spiritual Science.

The interest which was gradually being kindled in new aims for art was then overshadowed by the deteriorating world economic situation that set in a year later and the subsequent darkening political horizon. Thus sporadic articles in magazines, which in the 1930's acknowledged the new Goetheanum building – for example, in Great Britain –, often lacked a basis for the judgements offered. Without the support of any relevant aesthetic concepts, their authors were perplexed and made curious comparisons with organic creations. Thus the building on the hillside, which the American poet, Percy MacKaye, likened to the Phoenix in a sonnet in 1938, was compared with a toad by an English architect in 1930; and a South American said of the garret window in the Duldeck House, where he had spent the night, that he had 'slept in the brontosaurus's ear'! At all events the following decades witnessed a clarification as it were of the observers' own souls.

Dennis Sharp,[52] who has the credit of being the first openminded observer to devote a longer article to Rudolf Steiner's architecture, still hovers between a subjective and an objective approach. Thus he holds there to be amongst other things an 'erotic' trait in the Dornach buildings 'presumably characterizing their proximity to nature'! However this may be, his valuable contribution to contemporary architectural literature, which has found wide circulation in the western world owing to editions in Great Britain and the U.S.A., contains as the last chapter but one in *Modern Architecture and Expressionism*, 1966, the essay *Rudolf Steiner and the Way to a New Style in Architecture*. This had already been selected for separate publication three years earlier, as the editors felt that students in the South of England were ripe for a stimulus of this kind. (It may be concluded from the increasing number of final papers which since then have been submitted at architectural colleges far beyond the confines of Southern England, that this process of assimilation is in full swing. The distinguished American architectural critic, Henry Russell Hitchcock, has also commented on Rudolf Steiner's influence.)

Before some examples are cited to demonstrate the quality of the discussion of the Goetheanum and its architecture, it will surely be of interest if allusion is made to various themes which recur in essays on the subject.

The question of style is foremost. How are the Goetheanum and Rudolf Steiner, the architect, to be classified? The first to dispense with any form of labelling was Ilse Meissner-Reese[53] in a short but pertinent text to Clemens Kalisher's excellent illustrations of Dornach which appeared in 1965 in *Progressive Architecture*, the New York journal. The Goetheanum, which hitherto – and since – had nearly always been squeezed into 'Expressionism', even 'late German Expressionism', is here clearly termed 'unclassifiable'.

As Assia Turgenieff-Bugaieff[23] reports in the rewarding little book *The Goetheanum Glass Windows*, Rudolf Steiner himself saw the 'anthroposophical' style midway between Impressionism and Expressionism. This implies that it is just as appropriate to speak of architectural impressions as it is of expressionistic architecture in this connection.

A year after the publication of the Swiss edition of *Eloquent Concrete*, Wolfgang Pehnt's commendable book *The Architecture of Expressionism* appeared, which has since been published in English. A section of the long chapter, 'Development', has been devoted to 'Anthroposophical Architecture'. If Rudolf Steiner's architectural work is thus to be placed under any heading at all, Pehnt's choice certainly appears to be the most appropriate. The inaugurator of the style in question would certainly have taken no exception to this, provided it were not applied merely as a label.

Another theme recurring in architectural literature is the preoccupation with the Goetheanum's degree of 'modernity'. Imai, in his assessment, however, attaches no importance to this otherwise obstrusive concept. Indeed only those who have never really understood this building project as the solution to a new kind of planning task will continue to voice their opinion – not without complacency – that Rudolf Steiner would today design the building quite differently. What is not always realized – even on the part of anthroposophists – is that the outstanding merit of Steiner's architecture lies much more in the essential experience which his buildings evoke than in any particular details.

A further theme follows on from the last. Is

Rudolf Steiner, who had no 'office name-plate', to be classed as an architect at all? This question is answered mainly positively and with astonishment and admiration – almost envy, as in the case of Henry van de Velde. It must not be forgotten that some members of the 'guild' even called Le Corbusier an outsider after his death!

A theme of a different nature is the more or less outspoken discussion on the world of ideas underlying Goethean creative activity. It speaks in favour of all Steiner's architectural works (buildings as well as lectures on the subject) that his practical achievements are so impressed on the whole range that he cannot be reproached for divorcing theory and practice, as is all too often the case with individuals possessing a wealth of ideas – for example, Ruskin, and even Sullivan, to mention only the most eminent advocates of an achitecture founded on great moral ideas. On the contrary, one recognizes in Steiner that rare individuality who has succeeded in making practice and spiritual research harmonise, whereby his practice of art always preceeded any philosophical formulation.

Special attention must be drawn to the international character of the interest shown in the Goetheanum, as testified in professional literature throughout the world. Indeed, the most important and conscientious publications on Steiner as architect are at present appearing in the Far East. Following a well illustrated publication *Architecture as a Philosophy of Life: Rudolf Steiner* written by Yuji Agematsu,[54] the architect and lecturer on aesthetics, an illustrated volume on *Rudolf Steiner: The Artist*[55] by the same author is now being prepared for the press.

Besides the conscious appreciation of Steiner as a factor to be considered in the architectural development of the century, the equally conscious disregard must also be mentioned. This disregard, or even deliberate suppression of every mention of Steiner's activity, seems to stem from a sort of impotence; a reluctance on the part of the person concerned to class any architecture which merges with the sculptural in the mainstream of development. It is the opinion of such critics (which of course corresponds with their own interpretation of construction) that any further development can only proceed from a purely structural approach. Consequently, anthroposophical architecture does not meet the demands of this influential establishment. Those who are of like mind (but seldom put pen to paper!) have obviously not devoted enough time to a study of the Goetheanum building. Only time will tell which architectural style will in the final analysis go forth from this era as the authentic leading movement of the future. Two contrasting examples follow, to illustrate this tendency.

In Knaur's *Lexicon of Modern Architecture* (1963), reference is made to Steiner in four different places: apart from the introduction, above all under 'Reinforced Concrete' and under 'Expressionism'. On Page 258, we read: 'The plastic potentialities of concrete were fully developed in conformity with the requirements of German Expressionism in the cenotaph in Weimar by Gropius (1922) and the second Goetheanum in Dornach by Rudolf Steiner (1925-28)'. And on Page 86, alongside an illustration of the building: 'The Goetheanum in Dornach, which creates expressionistic effects in its pictorially meaningful layout, nevertheless stands apart in that it was designed in accordance with the religious convictions of Rudolf Steiner and Anthroposophy.'

After such precise statements it would be expected that three years later at least something similar would appear in every dictionary. But no! In 1966, Pevsner, Fleming and Honour accomplished the grotesque feat of not dedicating a single word or illustration to Steiner, Goetheanum or Anthroposophy in the entire volume of their *Penguin Dictionary of Architecture,* although around 1960 Sir Nikolaus Pevsner avowed at a meeting at Mackintosh's Glasgow School of Art that he still vividly remembered Rudolf Steiner's appearance at a lecture he had attended in his youth at the Architects' House in Berlin! In the extended German edition of this reference book, which appeared in 1971 as *Lexikon der Weltarchitektur* (Prestel Verlag), the publishers no doubt deemed it unfitting to refrain from any mention of Steiner altogether and seized upon an almost touching expedient. On Page 514, under the heading 'Switzerland', an illustration of the Goetheanum appears and, in connection with more recent developments in that country, the allusion is made: 'and also Expressionism in the years prior to and following the First World War is impressively represented (Goetheanum in Dornach by Rudolf Steiner, burnt down in 1913, reconstructed 1923-28)'.

A problem which nearly always presents the authors concerned with some difficulty is the chronology of the twentieth century, which after the shattering experiences of two world wars evidently does not appear continuous and consistent in the minds of younger research workers. Their confusion is revealed in a curious way in the case of Rudolf Steiner and his architecture. Up to the present day it is still suggested that he was possibly 'influenced' by Le Corbusier and Mendelsohn. It is simply overlooked that he was a whole generation older than they and that his spiritual roots – and fruits – were quite different ones. The correction of this error is accepted calmly enough, but the debaters in question are still not quite satisfied and reply that the anthroposophists obviously consider Rudolf Steiner to be utterly and uncontestably original! In the field of professional literature one frequently encounters an understandable sensitiveness in the face of certain anthroposophical publications which are considered too biased and propagandistic to enable the reader to form any judgement of his own. The anthroposophists are regarded as being too convinced that only they represent the truth. In this connection the allusion might be permitted that the discerning editor, author and architectural critic, Dr. Ulrich Conrads, to whom we owe many valuable publications, draws particular attention to the acceptable, unprejudiced tone of the (convinced!) authors in his positive review of *Sprechender Beton* ('Eloquent Concrete') in the Berlin journal *Bauwelt* in 1973. The authors were able to conclude from this that one of their hopes had been fulfilled.

Two further phenomena still demand attention. The first is the increasing number of treatises written on Rudolf Steiner, the architect, which are only of a semi-public nature. In 1977, four dissertations as well as numerous final papers by students in England, France, Germany, Sweden, Japan and North America were being prepared. The second phenomenon is precisely that which has *not* been written down and never will be. What Frank Lloyd Wright, Gropius, Le Corbusier and the younger Saarinen *thought* can only be surmised from their various remarks and from their proven acquaintance with Rudolf Steiner's achievements.

Let us now compare words from three different parts of the world concerning the second Goetheanum and its founder. In the west, Dennis Sharp[52] says: 'Steiner's architecture is really open sculpture; huge pieces of sculpture in which people move and have a new sense of being. This is what he intended. It is not sculptural building in the sense that Mendelsohn or Le Corbusier referred to in their equation of architecture with the magnificent play of light on form. It is rather an environment about and around which the primary spaces are created to invoke the response of the Spirit in man.' And four pages later: 'Almost immediately out of the conflagration arose a new and even more dynamic structure, Goetheanum II (begun in 1925), known affectionately to the adherents of Steiner's movement as The Building. This time it was more firmly constructed in reinforced concrete. Chronologically the two buildings indicate Steiner's progress as an architect. The experimental nature of the first building and the almost blind groping for the expression of new aesthetic laws give way to the imposing sculptural mass of the second.'

In central Europe, in the noteworthy critical discussion on *Anthroposophical Architecture,* already mentioned, Wolfgang Pehnt[19] reaches a climax in his text with the following words: ' "This modest spiritual home", as Rudolf Steiner's wife called the new House, is however in reality one of the grandest plastically architectural achievements of the twentieth century. Monumentality is attained in this case not by sheer bulk but by the way the mass is formed to implicate every detail. The compact exterior, the angular or curved surfaces leading on from one stratum to the next seem to obey a fluctuation of forces which partly break through from within and partly penetrate from without. The western façade powerfully piles up level upon level, as do the plastically less emphasized northern and southern wings. On the other hand, the shafts flanking the auditorium sink down like aerial roots. The groins and curves of the visible concrete surfaces remodel light every moment of the day from silvery grey to the deepest shade of black.'

And in the Far East the voice of Kenji Imai,

The Goetheanum, partial view from the south

who had once exclaimed on the terrace of the Goetheanum: 'You know Gropius? You know the "Bauhaus"? The architecture of functionalism! Steiner: the architecture of eternity! You see the whole cosmos come in!' In his account of 1964, when the impressions gained a year earlier were still fresh in his soul, he directs an appeal to humanity which is still valid and can therefore be offered to the public once again: 'I think it is our task to contemplate afresh the earnest spirit of Rudolf Steiner that indwells the Goetheanum architecture. I cannot help recognizing that his heart-felt desire to bring love and harmony to humanity, whereby the Goetheanum was to be a sun of peace, is beginning to shine as a great example to our modern architecture, just as he hoped. In this connection I must point to a peculiarity in all his work. With it the problem of tradition, which seems to dominate the minds of modern architects, recedes completely into the background. I appeal to architects throughout the world to make this Goetheanum building by Rudolf Steiner – the great philosopher of Spiritual Science, the artist with the mystical character, who is at the same time an architect – to make this building their present and future friend and to visit it at least once. My wish is that they may find an opportunity to ponder on the nature and value of this edifice and to recognize a genuine and dynamic achievement for what it is. In uttering this wish I will conclude my account.'[51]

There are still many aspects of the Goetheanum building impulse which have not been exhausted. It is to be expected that in years to come further writings will appear reflecting the architectural practice and experience of those who look up to the Goetheanum as their main source of inspiration.

The Eurythmeum, partial view from the north-east

The Eurythmeum, model by Rudolf Steiner   *The Eurythmeum, model by Rudolf Steiner*

RUDOLF STEINER'S CONTINUING ARCHITECTURAL IMPULSE

Nikolaus Ruff   Rex Raab

Spaces must be created for human life that correspond with its very being and action. This was the point of departure for Rudolf Steiner's architectural impulse. The building resulted from the requirements, town planning from the individual building. Practical building activity preceded Rudolf Steiner's lectures on architecture and accompanied them. Thus the development of this organically living architectural impulse did not take a theoretical or programmatical course for the architects who had accompanied it since 1907 in Munich and Dornach, but was of a practical and visible nature from the start. It developed from social circumstance and personal make-up and was influenced just as much by economic factors as it was derived from Rudolf Steiner's architectural abilities.

The first architects to experience the Dornach planning office and building sites, as well as Steiner's work and corrections, were largely those appointed by Rudolf Steiner himself, particularly for the assignments relating to the first and second Goetheanum. Nevertheless not only professionals were involved in the work but also amateurs who learnt on the site.

Independent or semi-independent projects in and outside Dornach during Rudolf Steiner's own lifetime were realized, for example, by Paul Bay in House Friedwart in Dornach (1921). The construction of the first Free Waldorf School in Stuttgart was commenced in 1923 under the direction of Weippert, company architect of the Waldorf-Astoria cigarette factory. Keeping to Rudolf Steiner's sketch designs, Schmid-Curtius executed the Eurythmeum and House del Monte, also in 1923 in Stuttgart.

Individual collaborators such as the architects Hermann Ranzenberger, Ernst Aisenpreis, Otto Moser and Albert von Baravalle remained in Dornach and continued their building activity there. As an amateur, the eurythmist, Mieta Pyle-Waller, was active at the Goetheanum in the construction of the cafe and restaurant (competition and execution in 1929-30), as was the stage designer and composer, Jan Stuten, who was involved with the interior decoration of the second Goetheanum (proposal for plastic work in the western staircase, which was not executed, but provided for) and in 1935-36 in the design of his own dwelling house (in collaboration with H. Ranzenberger).

Some architects adopted various aspects of this building impulse, for example, Montague Wheeler in England for the Rudolf Steiner Hall (1926) and Rudolf Steiner House (1931) in London, as well as for a cinema in Cambridge. Professor Benirschke, H. Ranzenberger and others projected building abroad, even overseas, which, although never executed, give evidence of Rudolf Steiner's incentives. In 1938, Mieta Pyle-Waller emigrated to the U.S.A. and is responsible for building projects in Spring Valley, New York, above all for the 'Auditorium' there.

A leading role amongst the generation born around the turn of the century is assumed by Helmuth Lauer, who became acquainted with the Goetheanum building site in his youth and gained practical experience in Paul Bay's office when the de Jaager House and the small transformer house in Dornach were being planned and executed. Subsequently he took the decisive step of settling down in Stuttgart where he soon emerged as designer of domestic and other buildings bearing their own independent stamp. The spark of enthusiasm had not been truly kindled within him until the design of the second Goetheanum had become known. He recognized in the Goetheanum building an expressive architecture which responded to the claims of the twentieth century as well as indicating those of the future. Since then he has above all gained a reputation as architect of chapels and churches for the Christian Community. It was his lot to witness how several of his buildings in Stuttgart were destroyed in the Second World War and only in part reconstructed. After the war, he bore the impulse to Scandinavia. Felix Kayser likewise became distinguished for his domestic buildings and publications. In The Hague, Holland, the Vrije School (1923) came into being, as well as the excellent Rudolf Steiner Kliniek (1929), by the architects J. W. E. Buys and Joan B. Dursen. However the Goetheanum architectural impulse did not generally flourish in the 30's and 40's, even if some buildings did demonstrate its continuation, as in England the Michael House School, Ilkeston, by Georg Nemes.

Amateurs assisted particularly in the interior decoration and furnishing of homes. Their participation has had a distinct meaning in the impulse's development, as not every architect would have had the courage to enter so uncompromisingly into the new world of form.

A younger generation was being trained and after the Second World War was gradually able to grow into the practice stimulated by Rudolf Steiner's initiatives. Meanwhile, the general situation had changed: more emphasis was being laid on the social significance of architecture in the face of the increasing anti-social effect of the built environment.

The older generation continued to receive stimulation from the impulses of the 20's. An interesting encounter of the two generations took place through the founding of the Stuttgart Anthroposophical Circle of Architects in 1947 and the correspondence 'Mensch und Baukunst' (Man and Architecture') in 1951 in the same circle launched by Wolfgang Gessner, Felix Durach and Felix Kayser.

A significant event in the development was the planning of an entire school complex for the Free Waldorf School in Rendsburg in 1950 by Felix Kayser. A part of this building project was realized immediately. (Kayser also constructed the large administrative building for the Electricity Board of Schleswig-Holstein in Rendsburg.) This complete school project implied the conquest of an entirely new dimension which was in keeping with contemporary requirements and heralded the possibilities of environmental planning inherent in this architectural impulse throughout the world. Rudolf Steiner once remarked: 'A school building is an artistically designed utility building.' The aim of architecture is not merely the realization of practical requirements: 'Architecture has to do with the same forces that shape the physical body of man. Man's present body is built according to the measurements prescribed by the ark and the Gothic cathedrals preformed the bodies of the mystics of the later Middle Ages. What our eyes perceive and our hands grasp thus works on into a distant future, moulding forms and shaping destiny. And it is not a matter of indifference if future forms, proportions and measurements are dictated by the purely utilitarian principles of present-day civilisation, which mean hindrance upon hindrance for what should come, or if corporeal forms are created that are in harmony with what ought to arise in the future.– And what applies to the microcosm has its corresponding implications for the macrocosm. We know we stand at a turning point in time that requires something exceptional of us. The destiny of whole worlds depends upon what we do. What we do is not a matter of indifference.'[56]

Nursery school buildings and teacher training centres followed on the school buldings as independent enterprises. Projects for curative centres ran alongside these which, particularly as a result of the rapid expansion of the world-wide 'Camphill Movement', were realized in many European countries, in South Africa and the U.S.A.

Arne Klingborg, initially involved in architectural assignments in Germany by Helmuth Lauer, advocates particularly convincingly the integration of the arts as it is contained in Rudolf Steiner's architectural impulse. The ethereal quality of colour is applied to interiors on a larger scale in the form of transparent or glazed surface treatment of various buildings, as in the Rudolf Steiner House, Stuttgart, in 1956-7, and altar-pieces for the Christian Community in Göppingen, Stuttgart and Berlin (1958-62). The travelling exhibition (Dornach, Berlin, London, etc.) in 1961, which formed part of the Rudolf Steiner centenary celebrations, was arranged by

Klingborg and also promoted the architectural impulse. As a result of this exhibition, Hans Scharoun became more closely acquainted with Rudolf Steiner's architecture and remarked: 'The Goetheanum is the most significant building of the first half of the century.' Later Scharoun designed a chapel for the Christian Community in Bochum.

Japan presents a chapter of its own. It begins in 1926 when the young Professor Kenji Imai from Tokyo was in Europe shortly after the opening of the new 'Bauhaus' in Dessau and visited the unfinished second Goetheanum in Dornach. Not until 1963 – thirty-seven years later – was he able to see the completed building.

Upon his return to Japan in 1963 Imai and his assistant, Ikehara, set about designing the 'Okuma Memorial Hall and Conference Centre', which receives its main source of inspiration from the Goetheanum architectural impulse. His student, Yuji Agematsu, also took an interest in Steiner's incentives and came to Europe. When he returned to Japan in 1969, he designed a doctor's house in central Japan on the basis of what he had learnt in Dornach and Engelberg. Largely in his literary works, Agematsu has become the main advocate of the Goetheanum architectural impulse in Japan.

The world situation today illustrates a differentiated practice. Rudolf Steiner called for diversity, individual design. The artistic basis of his new architectural impulse includes forms expressing various structural languages. Unity is created by the creative disposition, the method of attaining a functional form, the conception of metamorphosis and the organically living creative will. Thus this building conception may also be associated with endeavours by outstanding representatives of modern architecture: Mendelsohn, Aalto, Häring, Scharoun, Saarinen. Specific characteristics of individual schools of architecture and personal destinies are manifested in differences of design. Far too many contemporary architects throughout the world have adopted Rudolf Steiner's building conception to be able to mention all by name.

What has taken place in Dornach at the Goetheanum itself? The new beginning after the events of the 30's and 40's led to possibilities of recommencing work. In 1952: execution of the 'Foundation Stone Hall' by Albert von Baravalle; in 1956: interior completion of the Great Hall by Professor Johannes Schöpfer, Stuttgart. In 1962-64, Arne Klingborg and Rex Raab remodel the interior of the western section of the building; in 1968-69, the 'English Hall' in the south-east of the building is realized including murals, together with the new southern entrance vestibule (Raab). Since 1973 a general development plan for the Goetheanum site has become necessary, which is still being worked out as a special zone for the School of Spiritual Science.

With the appointment of Hans Hermann as Director of the Fine Arts Section at the Goetheanum in 1973, an increased activity with regard to architecture has arisen. Particularly in the form of regular conferences and exhibitions a considerable number of interested architects have been summoned to mutual research work and a necessary exchange of experiences.

As activities have increased, the tendency has developed of the client setting up his own building company. This does not only have economic motives or consequences. Building skills tend to be declining rapidly. The rebirth of architectural capacities can however proceed from the spirit of Rudolf Steiner's impulse. Emerson College (England) has founded its own building company, which already undertakes outside contracts. The collaboration of amateurs supports this tendency.

Training questions have become very acute. Apart from conferences and courses, there still exists no complete architects' training as Rudolf Steiner would have conceived it. For students seeking architectural impulses such as those encouraged by Rudolf Steiner, answers are needed to questions which arise in their practical activity. The contribution on the part of anthroposophists is assuming increasing importance and stimulating various universities to tread new ground. The Alanus College (Germany) is to extend its work in this direction and organize an academic year for students of Delft University, which is even to receive financial support from the authorities. The Rudolf Steiner Seminariet in Järna, Sweden, conducts an 'artistic line', which includes architecture, and at Emerson College conferences and courses are arranged by the group of architects there.

It is in the nature of the Goethean method that other professional fields are included in the training

The Goetheanum from the north

of architectural capacities. In this connection, reference is made to the annual week's anthropology course bearing on the sculptural, musical and speech elements in man, which is conducted by Dr. Gisbert Husemann.

In a situation which is still getting under way, public dissatisfaction with contemporary architecture has to be taken into consideration. This leads to the demand that citizens participate in planning and execution. *The Short Life of Modern Architecture,* a publication by Eberhard Schulz in 1977, articulates this awakening process in the face of architecture.

Many interested architects still have to forgo a methodical pursuit of Rudolf Steiner's designs and ideas before entering practice. Thus further training centres must necessarily be created.

In diverse publications of the architectural press over the past twenty years, Rudolf Steiner's buildings are considered as belonging to a rising modern architecture of the twentieth century. As opposed to the one-sidedness in many modern trends, its architectural versatility is being recognized now more than ever as better able than rigid geometrical grids to do justice to various design problems – hitherto primarily for education and remedial work.

The effect of Rudolf Steiner's impulse can be determined far beyond the discernible boundaries of anthroposophically oriented activity – as far as Frank Lloyd Wright and Walter Burley Griffin, who became a member of the Anthroposophical Society in Australia, and whose two colleagues, Lippincort and Eric Nicholls, continued their activity as anthroposophists in California and Sydney; and, similarly, amongst others, the younger Saarinen.

Immediate tasks are presented particularly in the field of domestic architecture and town planning, which anticipates a stimulus from Rudolf Steiner's conception of the tripartite division of the social organism. Interior painting in transparent colour ought to become more widespread as a factor exerting a considerable influence on the environment. Moreover, the furtherance of this architectural impulse very much depends on the solution of the problem of more mouldable form work for concrete, its surface treatment and a more satisfactory insulation of this material. A foundation enabling fundamental research work in a 'building yard' and at institutes for constructional physics would be required for this purpose.

Rudolf Steiner's expectations were set in many directions. Apart from appropriate cultural centres being established, he particularly hoped to lead technology with its one-sidedness and dangers back within human reach by an artistic shaping of the functional forms of industrial buildings in reinforced concrete. Here, too, architecture is presented with unlimited fields of activity and development, the solution of which will influence our future existence in one way or another.

The Practising Architect and the School for Spiritual Science at the Goetheanum

Christian Thal-Jantzen

By any standards Rudolf Steiner's work as an architect is remarkable and strikingly unusual. It is therefore not surprising that amongst those who have met his work there are both students and practising architects who wish to understand its origins. Nor, that there are those who, having reached a certain understanding of this, want to take this exploration further through their own practice of architecture.

It was out of the recognition of such needs in many spheres of life and work that the General Anthroposophical Society with the School for Spiritual Science within it was founded. The Society offers the opportunity for those who have an interest in insights which have arisen from spiritual scientific research both generally as well as in particular fields, whether it be architecture, medicine, education, economics, etc., to pursue it with others of similar interests in the same and other walks of life. The School, on the other hand, is there for those who wish to research these insights in their practical work. In order to do this an inner training is necessary which is offered within the General Anthroposophical Society. Further to this there are groupings of members of the School, according to their practical work in the world, known as Sections. These focus in the leadership of the respective Sections at the Goetheanum but are potentially at work wherever there are members of the School working together as such.

In Rudolf Steiner's architectural work, and in particular the first Goetheanum, one can see the possibility of architecture becoming again the mother of the fine arts; architecture in which all the arts find their reconciliation, enabled to work in harmony with one another, as can be experienced in the great architecture of the past. Then, harmony and artistic unity were possible through divine guidance, as for example described in the Old Testament with regard to the Temple of Solomon. Today there are no such priest-kings divinely inspired, and so we have the possibility of being directly responsible for what we create. Are we, however, exercising that responsibility if we do not find ways, appropriate for our time, to enable the divine to become active in human affairs, but now as co-workers so that the saying of the Christ may be realised: "Where two or more are gathered together in my name, there am I also."?

It is with such questions that architects come together at the Goetheanum for regular working meetings under the auspices of the Section for Visual Arts. These have included joint work with fellow sculptors and painters as well as collaboration with members of other Sections of the School. For example; "Architecture and etheric plant forms. Exercises in observation and comprehension of living nature as a path to develop new inner faculties" (with Natural Science Section); "Geometry in Architecture" (with Mathematical Section); "Exercises in music and architecture in relationship to human equilibrium" (with Medical Section).

It will be clear to the reader that the pursuit of architecture within the School of Spiritual Science involves a cultivation of new inner faculties and appropriate forms of co-working as a necessary pre-condition for creating an artistically integrated architectural setting for modern man.

Index of Architects

On the 8 July 1978 an exhibition was opened at the Goetheanum to celebrate the 50th anniversary of the inauguration of the second Goetheanum in 1928. The aim of the exhibition was to show something of Rudolf Steiner's architectural work, its art historical context and the work of architects who have attempted to develop Rudolf Steiner's approach to architecture in their own practice.

The following index includes all those architects who contributed to this exhibition but does not claim to cover all those who consider themselves part of the anthroposophical architectural movement which has arisen out of Rudolf Steiner's work. Except for the sixteen architects who had already died at the time the exhibition was being prepared, all those who exhibited were self-selective. All architects, lay and professional, known to have had connections with this movement were invited to submit work which they considered good examples of its aims.

Although not everything submitted was shown, at least one example from each architect who responded to the invitation was exhibited. Inclusion in this index is therefore simply a factual record and does not imply any judgement of either the architects or their work by the organisers or the Free School of Spiritual Science at the Goetheanum.

INDEX OF ARCHITECTS

Arne Klingborg
Åke Fant

Agematsu, Yuji
Matsudo, Japan 1942

Studies in architecture at Waseda University, Tokyo. 1967 Scholarship at the Goetheanum in Dornach, Switzerland. 1968 Assistant to Rex Raab, Engelberg, Germany. 1972 Enters the Ikehara Institute at Waseda University. Lecturer at Tokai University and at Waseda University in Tokyo. Publications: *Steiner's Art of the Goetheanum*, Geijutsushincho, 1970; *Architecture as a Philosophy of Life: Rudolf Steiner*. Tokyo, 1974; Japanese edition of Rudolf Steiner's *Ways to a New Style in Architecture*. Tokyo, 1977. Place of residence: Tokyo, Japan.

Aisenpreis, Ernst
Stuttgart 1884 – 1949 Dornach, Switzerland

Active in the planning office at the Goetheanum during the construction of the first and second Goetheanum. Works incl: timber house for Ita Wegman, 1924, and timber house belonging to the Ita Wegman Clinic, Arlesheim, 1928; Eurythmeum Extension, Dornach, 1935, in collaboration with Albert von Baravalle; House Jevsiejenko, House Mollwo, Dornach, Switzerland.

Alberts, Antonio
Milan 1927

Works: Wijkcentrum, Meerzicht, Zoetermeer. Place of residence: Amsterdam, Holland.

Alberts, Emmaus Church, Nijmegen

Andersen, Jan Arve
Tromsö, Norway 1947

Studies at Oslo School of Architecture. Co-founder with O. R. Nygaard and E. Tharaldsen of the 'Hus' group. Works: family house, 'Henrik Wergeland', in the Vidaråsen Settlement for the Handicapped. Place of residence: Bergen, Norway.

Asmussen, Rudolf Steiner Seminariet, Järna

Asmussen, Erik
Copenhagen 1913

1932 – 1937 Studies at Copehagen Polytechnic and School of Art. Activity in several architects' offices in Copenhagen, Aarhus and since 1939 in Stockholm. Collaboration with Nils Tesch. Since 1960, independent office. Works: Kristofferskolan, Stockholm; institute and domestic buildings for the Rudolf Steiner Seminariet in Järna, Sweden; Waldorf Schools in Järna, Copenhagen and Odense; students' hostel and workshops for an agricultural college in Norway; school hostel and workshops for Peredur Home School in England; designs for interior decoration, furniture and light fittings. Place of residence: Järna, Sweden.

Austin, David N. S.
England 1947

1966-72 Studies in architecture at Brighton College of Art. Collaboration in architects' offices in London and Belfast. 1976 Co-founder of the Thal-Jantzen, Mosbaek, Cooper, Austin Partnership, Forest Row. Works: Eurythmy-House, Emerson College; Eurythmy rooms and laboratories, Elmfield School. Place of residence: Forest Row, Sussex, England.

Baravalle, Albert von
Vienna 1902

1920 Participation in the wood-carving on the facade of the first Goetheanum Building. 1921-24 Studies in architecture at the Polytechnic in Stuttgart. 1924-28 Assistant in the planning office at the Goetheanum in Dornach. 1926-27 Site supervision of form work for the west front of the second Goetheanum. Since 1931,

Baravalle, Hofmann House, Dornach

chartered architect in Dornach. Works on reconstructions of Rudolf Steiner's plans and models. Works: 1953 extension of the Foundation Stone Hall in the second Goetheanum Building. Domestic buildings in Dornach, Arlesheim: Berger, Baravalle, Mollwo, Hofmann, Hammacher, Wolf. 1951 Weleda AG, Arlesheim, second construction phase. Place of residence: Dornach, Switzerland.

Balcke, Christian

Works: Braunschweig Civic Hall. Place of residence: Kassel, Germany.

Bay, Friedwart House, Dornach

Bay, Paul Johann
Oberdiesbach, Switzerland 1889 – 1952 Aberdeen, Scotland

Assistant in the planning office at the Goetheanum. Works: Friedwart House, 1921, in collaboration with Rudolf Steiner; execution of designs by Rudolf Steiner, together with Edith Maryon: House de Jaager and dwelling for Eurythmists, 1920-22; Haldeck House, 1924; old canteen (former hostel), 1925, Dornach, Switzerland.

Bayes, Kenneth
Fenny Stratford, England, 1911

Studies in architecture at Birmingham School of Art. ARIBA. Partner in the Design Research Unit, London. Co-founder with Sandra Francklin of the Environmental Centre for the Handicapped, London. Place of residence: Aurignac, Montaigny de Quercy, France.

Beck, Walter
Munich 1903

Studies in architecture at Munich Polytechnic, diploma in 1926. Practice in various architects' offices. Since 1932, independent architect in Erfurt. Works: domestic and industrial buildings, cinemas, Waldorf Schools in Munich, Nürnberg, Marburg, Frankfurt/M., kindergarten in Augsburg, Germany.

Bieri, Arthur
Berne 1915

Training as architect HTL in Burgdorf. Since 1945, independent office in Huttwil. Works include: dwelling with office; Marianus Hall in Berne, in collaboration with others. Chapel of Rest in Huttwil, together with Fini Klaar and Willi Hege. Rudolf Steiner School in Berne. Place of residence: Huttwil, Switzerland.

Biesenthal, Klaus
Pforzheim, Germany

Works: domestic buildings; Rudolf Steiner School, Berlin.

Billing, Peters and Ruff, teacher training college, Stuttgart

Billing, Johannes
Karlsruhe 1930

Studies at the State School of Architecture in Stuttgart. Collaboration with Hermann Billing in Stuttgart and vicinity. Since 1964, office with J. Peters and N. Ruff. 1967 Awarded the Paul Bonatz Prize for Architecture; 1969 the Hugo Häring Prize awarded to the office; 1977 further distinction for the festival hall of the Free Waldorf School in Stuttgart, Uhlandshöhe. Works: teacher training college for the Union of Waldorf Schools, Stuttgart, in collaboration with Prof. R. Gutbrod; Rural Education Centre, Wildberg; various domestic buildings; festival hall of the Waldorf School, Stuttgart, Uhlandshöhe; various branches of the Landes-Girokasse, Stuttgart; Church of the Christian Community, Ulm; Free Waldorf School, Ulm. Place of residence: Stuttgart, Germany.

Bockemühl, Community Hospital, Herdecke

Bockemühl, Gundolf
Dresden-Loschwitz 1925

1946-51, Studies in architecture at Dresden Polytechnic. Diploma under Richard Döcker. Chartered architect since 1953. Works: domestic and industrial buildings; Friedrich Husemann Clinic in Buchenbach; curative centre in Kassel; Hibernia School, Wanne-Eickel; students' halls of residence: community hospital in Herdecke. Since 1970, Bockemühl and Partner. Place of residence: Kemnat, near Stuttgart, Germany.

Boese, Herbert
Berlin 1909

Studies in architecture under Paul Bonatz in Stuttgart. 1936 diploma. Participation in competitions for school construction. Works: domestic buildings and school hostels. Place of residence: Tübingen, Germany.

Boos, Wilfried
Neuchâtel, Switzerland, 1921

Training as architect HTL with diploma. Plastic studies under Oswald Dubach and Carl Kemper in Dornach. Since 1946, independent office. Works: domestic, exhibition, sport and industrial buildings, cinemas. Publication: *Rudolf Steiner School Buildings*. Place of residence: Basle, Switzerland.

Bowman, Waldorf School, Toronto

Bowman, Dennis
Ontario, Canada

Work: Waldorf School, Toronto.

Buys, J.W.E.
Holland 1889

Works: Rudolf Steiner Kliniek in The Hague, together with Joan B. Lursen, 1929.

Chase, Herbert S.
USA

1967-72, Studies in architecture at Cincinnati University. 1973-76, Collaboration in Thal-Jantzen Associates, Forest Row, England. Since 1976, collaboration with Roy Olsen, Vancouver, Canada. Place of residence: Vancouver, Canada.

Cooper, Anthony E.
England 1946

1964-70, Studies in architecture at Canterbury College of Art. Collaboration in architects' offices in London. Since 1973, chartered architect. 1972 Lectureship in architecture at Canterbury College of Art. 1976 Co-founder of the Thal-Jantzen, Mosbaek, Cooper, Austin Partnership, Forest Row. Works: Eurythmy House, Emerson College; Eurythmy rooms and laboratories, Elmfield School. Place of residence: Forest Row, Sussex, England.

Devaris-Manteuffel, Barbara
Poland 1932

Studies in architecture at the Polytechnics of Warsaw, Poland, and Lucerne, Switzerland. EPUL-SIA, RIBA. Works: domestic buildings in Switzerland, France and Greece; industrial buildings

Devaris and Manteuffel, Michael Hall School, Forest Row

in Ghana, Nigeria and Spain; schools in England for the Waldorf School movement and remedial homes. Place of residence: Forest Row, Sussex, England.

Devaris, Denis
Athens 1929

Studies at the Universities of Athens and Lucerne, Switzerland. EPUL-SIA, TEE. Activity in Switzerland, France, Sweden, Greece, Ghana, Nigeria, England, Teneriffa and Kenya. Lecturer at the University of Nairobi, Kenya. Place of residence: Forest Row, Sussex, England.

Durach, crystallisation laboratory, Dornach

Durach, Felix
Stuttgart 1893 – 1963 Lörrach

1920-21, Assistant in P. J. Bay's office in Dornach. Works include: House Farbentor and crystallization laboratory in Dornach; 1962 execution of the south-west foyer in the second Goetheanum.

Dubach, Oswald
Russia 1884 – 1950 Dornach, Switzerland

Sculptor, teacher at the Sculpture School at the Goetheanum. Co-worker in the planning office at the Goetheanum. Collaboration in carving the first Goetheanum. Final model for the substructure of the second Goetheanum.

Ebbell, Ole Falk
Trondheim, Norway, 1879-1969 Berne

1900 Engineering examinations in Trondheim. Further studies at Dresden Polytechnic. From 1913 active in the Basle Building Society, from 1919 free-lance constructional engineer in Basle. Specialist in statics and reinforced concrete construction. Responsible for the statics and construction of the chief buildings on the Dornach hill. Works include: ward block of the City Hospital in Basle; factories in Basle and Alsace; statics and construction work on the second Goetheanum in Dornach, until 1952.

Ebinger, Wolfgang
Göppingen, 1930

Studies in architecture at the Polytechnic in Stuttgart. Diploma in 1958. Assistant to various architects in Frankfurt. Since 1968, partnership with Günter Lange. Works: German Embassy in Afghanistan; alterations to the chapel of the Christian Community, Frankfurt; Filstal Waldorf School, Göppingen-Faurndau. Place of residence: Frankfurt, Germany.

Fulgosi, Federico
Bergamo, Italy, 1938

Studies in architecture in Florence until 1965. Collaboration in the architects' office, 'Plastic-Organic Building', Stuttgart. Since 1971, active in the Atelier d'Architecture in Saint-Prex. Place of residence: Saint-Prex, Switzerland.

Gerritsen, Frits
The Hague, 1899-1944, Holland

Works: Domestic buildings in collaboration with Chris Wegerif; school for the association 'De Vrije School', The Hague, 1924.

Goebel, Carl-Lutz
Hamburg 1921

Diploma at the Polytechnic in Munich. Since 1955, chartered architect. Works: domestic buildings, small clinics and rural industrial buildings; girls' hostel; festival hall; special home school for curative centre, 'House Hohenfried', in Bayerisch-Gmain, Germany. Place of residence: Marquartstein, Germany.

Griffin, Walter Burley
Maywood, Illinois, USA 1876 – 1937 Lucknow, India

1899 Degree in architecture at the University of Illinois. Assistant in various architects' offices. 1900-1905, with Frank Lloyd Wright in Chicago and subsequently chartered architect in Steinway Hall. Commissions in the USA and Germany. 1912 First prize for the planning of Canberra in Australia. 1913-16, Architect-in-charge of construction in Canberra. Works: domestic, industrial and administrative buildings in Australia.

Griffin, University, Melbourne

Gutbrod, Rolf
Stuttgart 1910

1929-35, Studies in architecture at the Polytechnics of Berlin and Stuttgart. Since 1945, chartered architect in Stuttgart. 1947 Lecturer for design at Stuttgart Polytechnic. 1953 Appointment as university lecturer in Stuttgart. 1968 August Perret Prize of the Union Internationale des Architectes. 1970 Paul Bonatz Prize for the training-college building of the Union of Free Waldorf Schools in Stuttgart. 1972 Hugo Häring Prize and Paul Bonatz Prize. Works: concert hall in Stuttgart; banking and industrial buildings in Stuttgart; congress centre in Mecca; festival hall of the Free Waldorf School, Kräherwald, Stuttgart; Free Waldorf School in Wuppertal, together with Professor W. Henning and Professor W. Widdern, etc., etc. Place of residence: Berlin, Germany.

Gutbrod, Congress Centre, Mecca

Harnest, Almuth
Eislingen 1935

Studies in architecture at the Polytechnics of Stuttgart and Munich. Assistant in various architects' offices. Collaboration with Billing, Peters and Ruff in Stuttgart. Since 1968, chartered architect in Münster. Works: church and dwelling for the Christian Community in Ulm, in collaboration with Billing, Peters and Ruff. Place of residence: Münster, Germany.

Hermann, Edmund
Reutlingen 1942

Studies in architecture in Stuttgart. Activity with Beck-Erlang and Lee Stuttgart/Berlin. Landscape gardening with Professor Mattern. Since 1974, chartered architect. Works: domestic buildings, community centres, terrace houses; hotels and private residence for the Sultanate of Oman. Place of residence: Pliezhausen, Germany.

Houte de Lange, Fulco Carel, ten
Holland 1916

1938 Studies at Utrecht School of Agriculture. 1942 Architect ETH, Zurich. Activity in various architects' offices in Switzerland. 1947 collaboration in Bureau Stuivinga en ten Houte de Lange in Ziest; 1950 independent office. Since 1966, collaboration with van der Pluijm. Works: domestic buildings, schools, office buildings; industrial buildings; hospital; buildings for curative centres. Place of residence: Zeist, Holland.

Hupkes, Church of the Christian Community, Rotterdam

Hupkes, H.
Rotterdam 1920

Studies at Amsterdam School of Architecture. Works: church buildings in Holland, including churches for the Christian Community in Amsterdam, Rotterdam and Zeist. Place of residence: Amsterdam, Holland.

Ijzerlooij, Jacobus C. van
Holland 1925

1958 Studies in architecture at Delft Polytechnic. Works include: Church for Glencraig Curative Schools, Ireland. Place of residence: Bosch en Dum, Bilthoven, Holland.

Ikehara, cemetary chapel, Tokorozawa

Ikehara, Yoshiro
Tokyo 1928

Studies in architecture at Waseda University in Tokyo until 1951. 1953 Assistant in Yamashita-Architects' Office in Tokyo. Lecturer at the Imai Institute of Waseda University. 1971 Professorship at Waseda University. 1971 First prize in the competition, 'Fontivegge Business Center', in Perugia, Italy. Works: Nakayama House, Shizuka; Shirama Secondary School, Shirama; chapel in Tokorozawa Cemetery, Tokorozawa; Omiya Building, Yokosuka; Shoida House, Katsura. Publication: *Rudolf Steiner and the Goetheanum*, 1966. Place of residence: Tokyo, Japan.

Imai, Kenji
Tokyo, 1895

Studies in architecture at Waseda University in Tokyo until 1919. 1926 Tours Europe and studies Gaudi's buildings in Barcelona and those of Rudolf Steiner in Dornach. 1937 Professorship at Waseda University. 1963 Travels to Europe for the tenth anniversary of 'Amigos Gaudi' in Barcelona; visits Dornach. Works include: Waseda University Library, 1925; remembrance hall and church, Nagasaki, 1963; music hall for the Queen's 60th birthday, Tokyo, 1966; Toyama Museum, Kawastrimamura, 1970. Various distinctions from the Architectural Institute of Japan and the Japanese Academy of Art. Publications: *On the New Goetheanum Building,* Shinkogeijutsu, 1930; *Architecture and Humanity,* Tokyo, 1954; *Sketches on the European Tour,* Tokyo, 1964; *Rudolf Steiner and his Work – On the Goetheanum,* Kindaikenchiku, 1964. Place of residence: Tokyo, Japan.

Imai, Okuma Memorial Hall, Saga, Japan

Jacobson, David
Perth, Australia, 1951

Studies in architecture at the University of Sydney. Works include: kindergarten for Lorien Novalis School, Sydney, 1978. Place of residence: Lavender Bay, Australia.

Jacobson, Lorien Novalis School, Sydney

Karsten, Jürgen
Hamburg 1925

1945-47, Joiner's apprenticeship, 1947-50, Hamburg School of Architecture. Activity in various architects' offices in Germany. Since 1959, independent office in Hamburg. Works: curative children's home and school, Friedrichshulde, near Hamburg; church and community centre for the Christian Community in Hamburg-Volksdorf, together with G. Bockemühl and G. Schmidt-Bardorf; kindergarten; old people's home,

'Tobiashaus', belonging to the Grell-Foundation in Ahrensburg, near Hamburg, in collaboration with W. Roggenkamp. Further domestic and industrial buildings. Place of residence: Hamburg, Germany.

Kasbergen, Arie
Holland 1931

Works include: Rudolf-Steiner-Kindergarten, Voorschoten, Holland, 1978. Place of residence: Krimpen aan den Ijssel.

Kayser, villa, Stuttgart

Kayser, Felix
Milan 1892

Studies at the Polytechnics of Berlin, Munich and Dresden. Diploma in Dresden in 1916. Assignment in various architects' offices in Nürtingen and Stuttgart. Since 1927, independent office in Stuttgart. Works include: boarding school, 'Schloss Hamborn', near Paderborn; dwelling in Pforzheim. Place of residence: Kirchzarten, Germany.

Keller, Marwitz House, Dornach

Keller, Walter
Zurich 1928

Draftsman's apprenticeship in Zurich until 1947. 1952 Sculptor's training in Dornach. Since 1954, independent architect in Dornach. Collaboration on the periodical, 'Mensch und Baukunst'/ 'Man and Architecture'. Works: dwellings for Brett, Grund, Marwitz in Dornach and for Aprile in Rome; kindergarten in Dornach. Place of residence: Dornach, Switzerland.

Kemper, Carl
Kharkov, Russia 1881 – 1957 Dornach, Switzerland

Art studies in Kharkov. Studies in architecture at the Polytechnic in Berlin. Studies in painting and sculpture in Paris and in the 'Jahrhundertwende-Atelier' in Munich. Meeting with Rudolf Steiner in Munich. Collaboration on the first Goetheanum from 1914; teacher at the Sculpture School in Dornach. Decisive contribution towards working out the west façade of the second Goetheanum after Rudolf Steiner's death.

Klein, Christian
1917

Studies in architecture in Stuttgart. 1945-61 Collaboration in Professor J. Schöpfer's office in Stuttgart. Since 1961, chartered architect. Works: domestic, industrial and school buildings and town planning. Kindergarten in Strasbourg; second extension of Weleda AG, Schwäbisch Gmünd; Free Waldorf School, Engelberg, in collaboration with Rex Raab; special school, 'Raphaelhaus', Stuttgart. Since 1973, partnership with Klaus Forgber. Place of residence: Stuttgart, Germany.

Kubiessa, Klaus
Elbing, Germany, 1933

Carpenter's apprenticeship. Training in several architects' offices. Specialized work on theatre construction. Since 1975, independent office. Works: Waldorf School in Lübeck. Place of residence: Nübbel, near Rendsburg, Germany.

Lane, Reuben
Sydney, Australia 1931

Training as architect and town planner in Australia. Activity in various architects' offices in Canada, USA, Mexico, Brazil, England and France. Work for the handicapped. Since 1968, independent office. Works: Waldorf Schools, Inala School and Warrah Cottage, Sydney. Place of residence: Sydney, Australia.

Lauer, Helmuth
Mühlheim a. D. 1901

Studies in architecture at the Polytechnic in Stuttgart and ETH Zurich. Diploma 1925. Assistant to Professor Abel and Professor Graupner, Stuttgart. Since 1929, independent architect.

Lauer, Church of the Christian Community, Stuttgart

1920-22 collaborator in 'Bay's Building Hut' in Dornach during the construction of the de Jaager House and the planning and execution of the transformer house, according to Rudolf Steiner's sketches. Works: clerical seminary for the Christian Community in Stuttgart, 1932; church building for the Christian Community in Stuttgart, 1938; further churches for the Christian Community; numerous school, hall, home and domestic buildings for Waldorf Schools, eurythmy and curative work. Place of residence: Stuttgart, Germany.

Laws, Nigel

Studies in architecture at the Northern Polytechnic, London. ARIBA, 1962. Assistant in various architects' offices: Eric Lyons, D. G. Joyce and D. S. Tucker. Since 1974, chartered architect. Works: industrial and administrative buildings; 'Michael Fields', Forest Row, Sussex, together with Prof. Kresse, Stuttgart, and Preben Jacobsen, Kent. Place of residence: Kent, England.

Leicht, Walter
USA 1921

Studies in architecture in New York. Collaboration with Gustav Iser. Works: Green Meadow Waldorf School, Eurythmy School, Weleda Building, domestic buildings in Spring Valley; various buildings for the Camphill Centres in the USA; chapel for the Christian Community, Devon, Penns. Place of residence: Spring Valley, USA.

Lürsen, Joan B.
Holland 1894

Works: Rudolf Steiner Kliniek te Den Haag, 1929, together with J.W.E. Buys.

Mosbaek, Jørn
Denmark 1938

1956-59 Mason's apprenticeship. 1963-68, Studies in architecture at the School of Art in Copenhagen. Collaboration in architects' offices in Copenhagen, Aarhus and Stockholm. Since 1972, collaboration with Thal-Jantzen in England. 1976 Co-founder of the Thal-Jantzen, Mosbaek, Cooper, Austin Partnership, Forest Row, England. Works: Eurythmy House, Emerson College; Eurythmy rooms and laboratories, Elmfield School. Place of residence: Forest Row, Sussex, England.

Moser, Moser House, Dornach

Moser, Otto
Stuttgart 1898 – 1966 Zurich

Collaboration in the planning office at the Goetheanum. Works: 1932 café and restaurant at the Goetheanum, together with M. Pyle-Waller; 1922-32, dwellings: von Baltz, Brons, Haldeck, Lewerenz, Moser, Wachsmuth, Zuccoli, in Dornach.

Moser, Hermann
Stuttgart 1890 – 1945 Stuttgart

Collaboration in the planning office at the Goetheanum during the construction of the second Goetheanum.

Müller, Fritz
Öhringen, Germany, 1906

Studies in architecture at Stuttgart Polytechnic. Since 1929, chartered architect. Works: numerous school buildings; co-workers' house at the Goetheanum; students' hall of residence at the Goetheanum, Dornach; Waldorf Schools in Pforzheim, Karlsruhe, Mannheim, Hannover, Stuttgart, Nürnberg; Free Youth Institute, Stuttgart; therapy wing of the Friedrich Husemann Clinic, Buchenbach-Wiesneck. Place of residence: Stuttgart, Germany.

Nemes, Agricultural and Cultural Education Centre, Fulenhagen

Nemes, Georg
Siebenbürgen 1900

Studies in architecture at the Polytechnic in Vienna. 1926 Collaboration in the building office at the Goetheanum. Activity in Vienna, England, Switzerland, France and Germany. Works: Agricultural and Cultural Education Centre, Fulenhagen. Place of residence: Öhningen, Germany.

Nygaard, Ole Rasmus
Bergen, Norway 1946

Studies at the School of Architecture in Oslo. Co-founder with Jan Arve Andersen and Espen Tharaldsen of the 'Hus' group. Works: family house, 'Henrik Wergeland', in the Vidaråsen-Settlement for the Handicapped. Place of residence: Oslo, Norway.

Ogilvie and Klein, Filder Clinic, Stuttgart

Ogilvie, Wilfried
Amsterdam 1929

Studies in painting and sculpture in Stuttgart and Munich. 1973 Co-founder of the Alanus College of Music and Fine Arts, Alfter, near Bonn. 1974 Founder of the Alanus Building Corporation. Works include: therapy centre and school premises. Place of residence: Alfter, near Bonn.

Peters, Jens
Hamburg 1934

Studies in architecture at the Polytechnic in Stuttgart. Diploma under Rolf Gutbrod, 1961. Assistant in various architects' offices in Hamburg, Basle and Helsinki. Since 1964, office with J. Billing and N. Ruff. Awarded the Paul Bonatz Prize for Architec-

Peters, Billing and Ruff, Waldorf School, Stuttgart

ture in 1967 and the Hugo Häring Prize for Architecture in 1969. Further distinction in 1977 for the festival hall of the Free Waldorf School, Stuttgart, Uhlandshöhe. Works: teacher training college of the Union of Waldorf Schools, Stuttgart, together with Prof. R. Gutbrod; Rural Education Centre, Wildberg; various domestic buildings; festival hall of the Waldorf School, Stuttgart, Uhlandshöhe; branches of the Landes-Girokasse, Stuttgart; Church of the Christian Community, Ulm; Free Waldorf School, Ulm. Place of residence: Stuttgart, Germany.

Plany, Egon
Schwerin, Germany, 1924

1947-57 Studies in architecture and painting in Berlin. Chartered architect and science assistant at the University of Technology in Berlin until 1965. Since 1964, cultural architectural work in Jerusalem; librarian for science at Hanover University Library. Place of residence: Hanover, Germany.

Podolinsky, Alexei de
1925

Self-taught. Works: Rudolf Steiner School and Kindergarten in Melbourne; Wandin Curative Home; domestic buildings in Wandin. Place of residence: Powelltown, Australia.

Podolinsky, kindergarten, Melbourne

Raab, Church of the Christian Community, Heidenheim

Pyle-Waller, Mieta
USA 1883 – 1952 USA

Works: House Pyle, 1927-31; café and restaurant at the Goetheanum, 1932, in collaboration with O. Moser. Auditorium, Spring Valley, NY, USA.

the Thal-Jantzen, Mosbaek, Cooper, Austin Partnership, Forest Row, England. Works: Eurythmy House, Emerson College; Elmfield School, Eurythmy rooms and laboratories. Place of residence: Forest Row, Sussex, England.

Pyle-Waller, cafe and restaurant, Dornach

Raab, Rex
London 1914

1931 Studies in architecture at the Northern Polytechnic, London. 1938 ARIBA. 1936-39 Studies at the Sculpture School at the Goetheanum, Dornach, under Oswald Dubach and Carl Kemper. Furniture designs for Messrs. Erwin Behr, Wendlingen, Germany. Since 1954, independent office in Engelberg. Works include: New Church of the Christian Community in Berlin, together with H. Lauer; Free Waldorf School, Engelberg; curative home, 'Ekkharthof', Lengwil, Switzerland. Dortmund Educational and Social Centre; extensions at the Goetheanum. Place of residence: Engelberg, Germany.

Ranzenberger, Weleda A.G. (first building) Arlesheim

Radysh, Wolodymyr
USA

1969 Studies in architecture at the University of the City of New York and the School of Architecture. Since 1976, co-worker in

Ranzenberger, Hermann
Stuttgart 1891 – 1967 Salzburg

Training as architect and sculptor in Stuttgart. 1914-29, Active as architect at the first and second Goetheanum and subsequently as chartered architect in Dornach. During the First World War, correction of his designs by Rudolf Steiner. Works include: Weleda AG; school for goldsmiths and jewellers, studio house, 'Hügelweg'; House Ranzenberger; House Messmer.

Rennert, Klaus
Berlin 1931

Carpenter's apprenticeship, Kassel State School of Architecture. Work in various architects' offices. Independent activity from 1963. 1970-73, partnership with Klaus Biesenthal. Works include: chapel for the Christian Community; Waldorf Kindergarten; hostel for the curative centre in Lauterbad, in collaboration with Klaus Biesenthal, Kassel; Waldorf Kindergarten in Siegen; Waldorf School for the Loheland Foundation in Künzell; hall for Rüspe Students' Hostel, Kirchhundem. Place of residence: Kassel, Germany.

Ris Allen, Joan de
Ridgewood, USA, 1931

Studies in architecture at Columbia University in New York City. RIBA, ARIAS. Assistant in the architects' office of Adams and Woodbridge, NYC. Chartered architect in South Egremont, Mass., USA. Since 1969, in Botton Village, Yorkshire, England. Co-founder of the Camphill Architects' Group, England. Works include: Camphill Village in Copake NY; Camphill Special Schools in Beaver Run, Penns.; Rainbow Hall; Fountain Hall; Phoenix Hall in Newton Dee; Tourmaline Hall in The Grange Village. Place of residence: Newton Dee, Bieldside, Aberdeen, Scotland.

Risseeuw, Joan
Oosterbeek, Holland

Works: Iona-gebouw for the Vrije Hogeschool, Driebergen; domestic buildings for curative centre, 'Michaelshoeve', Brummen, Holland.

Ruff, Peters and Billing, dwelling, Unterlengenhardt

Ruff, Nikolaus
Stuttgart 1934

Studies in architecture at the Polytechnics of Stuttgart, Berlin and Munich. 1960 Diploma under Rolf Gutbrod, Stuttgart. Activity in various architects' offices in Basle, Istanbul and Helsinki. 1961-64, collaborator in Rolf Gutbrod's office in Stuttgart. Since 1964, office with J.Billing and J.Peters. 1966-67 and from 1977, lecturer at the Polytechnic. 1967 Awarded the Paul Bonatz Prize for Architecture and the Hugo Häring Prize awarded to the office. 1977 Further distinction for the festival hall of the Free Waldorf School in Stuttgart, Uhlandshöhe; Works: teacher training college for the Union of Free Waldorf Schools in Stuttgart, together with Prof. R. Gutbrod; Rural Education Centre, Wildberg; various domestic buildings; festival hall of the Waldorf School, Stuttgart, Uhlandshöhe; various branches of the Landes-Girokasse, Stuttgart; Church of the Christian Community, Ulm; Free Waldorf School, Ulm. Place of residence: Stuttgart, Germany.

Schöpfer, Rosenthal House, Dornach

Schöpfer, Johannes
Stuttgart 1892 – 1961 Stuttgart

Studies at the Advanced School of Architecture in Stuttgart. Activity in various government departments. Independent office in 1945 with town-planning assignments relating to post-war reconstruction. 1945 Lecturer for design and housing at the State School of Architecture in Stuttgart; professorship in 1951. Works include: reconstruction of the Waldorf School, Haussmannstrasse, Stuttgart; first extension of Weleda AG, Schwäbisch Gmünd; interior completion of the Great Hall at the Goetheanum in Dornach; House Rosenthal, Dornach.

Scholl, Gerhard
Pforzheim 1915

Studies at the Polytechnic in Stuttgart, diploma in 1952. Collaboration in architects' offices. Since 1956, active independently in Pforzheim. Works: domestic, commercial and industrial premises; House Dr. Treiber in Wildbad, Black Forest; House Ulrich in Pforzheim; Kindergarten of the Waldorf School and Rudolf Steiner House in Pforzheim. Place of residence: Pforzheim, Germany.

Scholl, Rudolf Steiner House, Pforzheim

Seyfert, Werner
Stuttgart 1930

Studies in architecture in Stuttgart. In the mid-50s founder of the 'Plastic-Organic Building Group', Bureau Seyfert. Works: Free Waldorf School in Heidenheim; Free Waldorf School in Bremen. Place of residence: Stuttgart/Bernhausen, Germany.

Seyfert, special home school, Föhrenbühl

Stuhlmann, Erwin M.
Hamburg 1929

Mason's apprenticeship. Studies at the School of Architecture and Surveying in Hamburg. Since 1954, active in various architects' offices in Hamburg. Works: collaboration in church construction for the Christian Community and in various state school buildings in Hamburg. Place of residence: Hamburg, Germany.

Stuten, Jan
Nijmegen 1890 – 1948 Dornach, Switzerland

Work: design of House Stuten, 1937.

Tallo, Gabor
Brezno, Czechoslovakia, 1910-1978 Newnham-on-Severn, England

Studies in architecture in Ghent and Vienna. ARIBA, ARIAS, ISAA. 1931-33, Collaboration with Hermann Ranzenberger, Oswald Dubach and Carl Kemper in Dornach. Since 1933, chartered architect in Genoa, Italy, and later in Johannesburg, Pretoria and Capetown, South Africa. Since 1958, active for the Camphill Movement in Scotland. Co-founder of the Camphill Architects' Group. Works include: Murtle Hall in Camphill, Aberdeen.

Tallo, Myrtle Hall, Camphill Village, Aberdeen

Thal-Jantzen, Christian
Denmark, 1944

1964-70, Studies in architecture at London Polytechnic. Assistant in various architects' offices. Since 1971, chartered architect. Collaboration with Rex Raab for Emerson College. 1976 Co-founder of the Thal-Jantzen, Mosbaek, Cooper, Austin Partnership, Forest Row. Works: Eurythmy House, Emerson College; Eurythmy rooms and laboratories, Elmfield School. Place of residence: Forest Row, Sussex, England.

Tharaldsen, Espen
Jevnaker, Norway 1947

Studies at Oslo School of Architecture. Co-founder with J. A. Andersen and O. R. Nygaard of the 'Hus' group. Works: family house, 'Henrik Wergeland', in the Vidaråsen Settlement for the Handicapped. Place of residence: Bergen, Norway.

Thomassen, Eivind
Vinger, Norway 1914

Studies in architecture with diploma at Stuttgart Polytechnic, 1937. Chartered architect in Oslo, Norway.

Trouw, Herpert
Holland 1937

Studies in architecture HBO. Activity as town planner in Nijmegen. Works include: School for Bio-Dynamic Agriculture, Thedingsweert, Holland. Place of residence: Nijmegen, Holland.

Tschakalow, Arild curative home school, Bliestorf

Tschakalow, Alexander
Swischtew, Bulgaria, 1909

Studies in architecture at Stuttgart Polytechnic, diploma under Paul Bonatz. Since 1935, active in Stuttgart, later Basle. Course at the Sculpture School at the Goetheanum under Oswald Dubach. Since 1950, independent office in Dornach. Works: domestic buildings in Dornach; children's home, 'Sonnenhof', Arlesheim; Centre de Pédagogie Curative St. Prex; Association La Branche, Savigny; curative home school for maladjusted children, 'Arild', Bliestorf, near Lübeck; Renan Work Colony; children's home, 'Christofferus', Renan; curative home, 'Columban', Urnäsch, in collaboration with M. Ganz. Place of residence: Dornach, Switzerland.

Ulrich, Karl
Merazhofen, Germany, 1904

Studies in painting and sculpture. Work: Escola Higienopolis (Escola Rudolf Steiner), São Paulo, Brazil. Place of residence: Kirchzarten, Germany.

Waltjen, C.
Lindau, Lake Constance 1923

Studies in architecture at Munich Polytechnic. Centred on Frankfurt. Works: House Proels, 1975; Waldorf School, Bexbach, 1st construction phase 1976/77. Place of residence: Frankfurt, Germany.

Wegerif, Chris
Holland

Place of residence: Cape Town, South Africa.

Wheeler, Montague
England 1874 – 1937 London

1888-91 Studies at Marlborough College and Trinity Hall, Cambridge. Collaboration with Edward Basday House in London from 1898 to his death in 1937. Works: Rudolf Steiner Hall (1926); Rudolf Steiner House (1931), London.

Wheeler, Rudolf Steiner House, London

Zimmer, Erich
Karlsruhe 1924-1976 Arlesheim

Studies in architecture at the Polytechnic in Karlsruhe, diploma in 1949. Assistant in various architects' offices. Chartered architect in Dornach as from 1966. Works: various domestic buildings in Dornach and Arlesheim; Eurythmy Hall. Publications: Co-writer of *'Das zweite Goetheanum und der Baugedanke'* ('The Second Goetheanum and Its Conception'), Stuttgart, 1965; from 1967 editor of the anthroposophical architectural periodical, *'Mensch und Baukunst'* ('Man and Architecture'); *'Rudolf Steiner als Architekt von Wohn- und Zweckbauten'* ('Rudolf Steiner – Architect of Domestic and Utility Buildings'), Stuttgart, 1971; *Der Baugedanke von Malsch und das erste Goetheanum* ('The Malsch Building Conception and The First Goetheanum'), Stuttgart, 1978.

Zimmer, Hulton House, Arlesheim

THE DORNACH BUILDING CHRONICLE

FIRST CONSTRUCTION PERIOD

1913	July	Interior model of the 1st Goetheanum
1913	20 September	Laying the foundation stone
1914	1 April	Topping-out ceremony
1914	14 July	Inauguration of the 'Glashaus'
1915		Opening of the 'Heizhaus'
1915-16		'Haus Duldeck'
1914-18		Work slows down on the 1st Goetheanum during the First World War
1920	September	Opening of the 1st Goetheanum (still incomplete)

SECOND CONSTRUCTION PERIOD

1919-21		Vreede Residence, Arlesheim
1919-20		Studio House van Blommestein
1920-21		Three 'Eurythmy Houses'
1921-22		Studio House de Jaager
1921		Friedwart Residence. Responsible: Paul Bay
1921		Transformer House
1922	New Year's Eve	1st Goetheanum destroyed by fire

THIRD CONSTRUCTION PERIOD

1923-24		'Eurythmeum'
1923-24		Extensions to 'Haus Brodbeck'
1923-24		Publishing house
1924	mid March	Exterior model of the 2nd Goetheanum
1924	9 September	Building approval
1924-25		Site cleared and construction work commences
1924-25		Haus Schuurman
1925	30 March	Death of Rudolf Steiner
1926	29 September	Topping-out ceremony
1927	29 September	The wooden statue is erected in the eastern part of the building
1928	29 September	Opening of the 2nd Goetheanum (still unfinished)
1930		Southern staircase and southern vestibule. Responsible: Carl Kemper
1935	Easter	Completion of the space for the wooden statue Design Mieta Pyle-Waller, O. Moser
1935-36		Alterations and extensions to the 'Rudolf Steiner-Halde' (former 'Haus Brodbeck'). Responsible: Ernst Aisenpreis

FOURTH CONSTRUCTION PERIOD

1952		Completion of the former rehearsal stage on the ground floor as hall for 500 persons, with its own stage (Foundation Stone Hall). Responsible: Albert von Baravalle
1956-57		Completion of the 'Great Hall'. Responsible: Johannes Schöpfer
1957	Easter	Opening of the completed 'Great Hall'
1962-64		Western projection. Responsible: Rex Raab and Årne Klingborg
1964	Michaelmas	Opening of the western entrance
1969-71		South-eastern projection. Alterations to the south portal and southern vestibule. Creation of the 'English Hall'. Responsible: Rex Raab.
1971	Autumn	Wall murals in the 'English Hall': Gerard Wagner

Where not otherwise stated, designs by Rudolf Steiner were executed during the first, second and third construction periods.

BIBLIOGRAPHY

RUDOLF STEINER

1888, 9 November
Goethe as Founder of a New Science of Aesthetics, Anthroposophical Publishing Co., London, 1922.

1907, 13 September
The Creative Cosmic Tone, lecture in *Occult Signs and Symbols,* Anthroposophic Press, New York 1972.

1909, 28 October
The Being of the Arts, in *1979 Golden Blade,* Rudolf Steiner Press, London, 1979.

1909
Occult Science – An Outline, Chapter IV: Man and the Evolution of the World; Rudolf Steiner Press, London, 1979.

1911, 12 December
And the Temple Becomes Man, Rudolf Steiner Press, London, 1979.

1914, 23 January
Über die Anthroposophenkolonie in Dornach.

1914
Ways to a New Style in Architecture, Anthroposophical Publishing Co., London, 1927.

1914
Der Dornacher Bau als Wahrzeichen künstlerischer Umwandlungsimpulse, Dornach, 1937.

1914, 28 December
Technology and Art, in *1959 Golden Blade,* Rudolf Steiner Press, London, 1959.

1914, 29 & 30 December
Kunst im Lichte der Mysterienweisheit, partially translated in *Art in the Light of Mystery Wisdom,* Rudolf Steiner Press, London, 1970.

1916, 11 January
The Mission of Spiritual Science and of Its Building at Dornach, Switzerland, (published by) H. J. Heywood-Smith, London, 1917.

1916, 20 September
Architectural Forms Considered as the Thoughts of Culture and World-Perception, Rudolf Steiner Publishing Co., London, (no date).

1918, 15 January
Wesen und Bedeutung der illustrativen Kunst, Dornach, 1940.

1918, 5 May
Die Quellen der künstlerischen Phantasie und die Quellen der übersinnlichen Erkenntnis, in *Kunst und Kunsterkenntnis,* Dornach, 1961.

1919, 28 October
Cultural Questions, in *The Social Future,* Anthroposophic Press, New York, 1972.

1920, 8 September
Die zwölf Sinne des Menschen in ihrer Beziehung zu Imagination, Inspiration und Intuition, in *Geisteswissenschaftliche Erkenntnis der Grundimpulse sozialer Gestaltung,* Dornach, 1967.

1920, 12 September
The Supersensible Origin of the Artistic, in *Art in the Light of Mystery Wisdom,* Rudolf Steiner Press, London, 1970.

1920
Der Baugedanke von Dornach, Dornach, 1942.

1921, 29 June
The Architectural Conception of the Goetheanum, Rudolf Steiner Publishing Co., London, 1938 (to be used with illustrations from *Der Baugedanke des Goetheanum,* Dornach, 1932.).

1921, 29 July
Architektonische Stilfragen, in *Die Drei* 1930/31, 10th Year, Book 7.

1921
Stilformen des Organisch-Lebendigen, Dornach, 1933.

1922, 7–12 April
Die Bedeutung der Anthroposophie im Geistesleben der Gegenwart, Dornach, 1957. Of these six lectures, two have been published in English in the *1961 Golden Blade:*
8 April   The Position of Anthroposophy among the Sciences.
9 April   Anthroposophy and the Visual Arts.

1923, 7 January
Die Herz-Erkenntnis des Menschen, in *Lebendiges Naturerkennen – intellektueller Sündenfall und spirituelle Sündenerhebung,* Dornach, 1966.

1923, 19 January
Truth, Beauty, Goodness, in *Art in the Light of Mystery Wisdom,* Rudolf Steiner Press, London, 1970.

1923, 18 May – 9 June
The Arts and Their Mission, Anthroposophic Press, New York, 1964.

1924
Der Wiederaufbau des Goetheanums, in *Der Goetheanumgedanke inmitten der Kulturkrisis der Gegenwart (Gesammelte Aufsätze),* Dornach, 1961.

OTHER AUTHORS

AGEMATSU, YUJI
Steiner's Art at the Goetheanum. *The Geijutsu-Shincho,* No. 4/1971, Tokyo.

ARCHITECTURAL DESIGN
Concrete Interlude, July 1971, London.

ARCHITECTURAL FORUM
An Architect's Scrapbook: The secret dossier of an architectural scavenger, New York, 1964.

ARCHITECTURAL INSTITUTE OF JAPAN, TRANSACTIONS OF
On the Architecture of Rudolf Steiner, No. 186/1971, Tokyo.

ARCHITECTS
Rudolf Steiner's Architecture. No. 26/1963, Copenhagen.

BÜCHER, MAX and ERWIN HEINLE
Building in visual concrete, Technical Press, London.

BARAVALLE, ALBERT
Das Goetheanum in Dornach, in *Schweizerische Technische Zeitschrift,* No. 42/1945. Das Form-Motiv des Zweiten Goetheanum, in *Das Goetheanum,* No. 12, 31st Year, 1952.

BAUWELT 1962
Diskussion über das Westtreppenhaus des zweiten Goetheanums.

BAYES, KENNETH
Architecture in accord with Man, in *The Faithful Thinker: Centenary Essays on the Work and Thought of Rudolf Steiner,* Hodder and Stoughton, London, 1961.

BIESANTZ, HAGEN
Rudolf Steiner als denkender Künstler, in *Das Goetheanum,* Vol. 54, no.13, 1975, Special Number commemorating the fiftieth anniversary of Rudolf Steiner's death.

BONFANTI, ENZIO and MARIO PORTA
L'architettura: Fondazione del movimento moderno, in *L'Arte moderna,* No. 123, Vol. XIV, Milan, 1967.

BOOS-HAMBURGER, HILDE
The Creative Power of Colour, The Michael Press, London 1976.

BRION-GUERRY, L.
L'Année 1913, Vol. 2, Editions Klincksieck, Paris, 1971.

BRUNATO, MARIO and SANDRO MENDINI
L'Architettura, Nos. 55, 56, 57, 58. Rome 1960.

CONRADS, ULRICH and H. H. SPERLICH
Ueber Steiners Dornacher Bauten, in *Phantastische Architektur,* Ullstein, Berlin, 1960.

FANT, ÅKE, ARNE KLINGBORG and A. JOHN WILKES
Rudolf Steiner's Sculpture in Dornach, Rudolf Steiner Press, London, 1975.

FIECHTER, ERNST
Zum Neubau des Goetheanums bei Dornach, in *Schweizerische Bauzeitung,* Vol. 85, No. 7/1925.

GESSNER, WOLFGANG
Die Sprache der Baukunst, Raum und Gebärde, Verlag Freies Geistesleben, Stuttgart, 1948.
Baukunst in der Wende der Zeit, Verlag Freies Geistesleben, Stuttgart, 1956.
Das zweite Goetheanum und der Baugedanke, Verlag Freies Geistesleben, Stuttgart, 1965.

GOETHE, WOLFGANG VON
The Metamorphosis of Plants, with an Introduction by Rudolf Steiner, Bio-Dynamic Literature, Wyoming 1974.
Theory of Colours, MIT Press.

GUBLER, JACQUES
Beton et architecture, Trois propositions des années 1925, in *Werk,* 55/1971, Zurich.

HARTMANN, GEORG
The Goetheanum Glass-Windows, Philosophisch-Anthroposophischer Verlag, Dornach, 1972.

HEMLEBEN, JOHANNES
Rudolf Steiner, Henry Goulden Ltd., East Grinstead, 1976.

HITCHCOCK, HENRY-RUSSELL
Architecture – Nineteenth and Twentieth Centuries, Penguin Books, London, 1958.

IKEHARA, JOSHIRO
Introducing Eminent Works, Goetheanum at Dornach, in *Space Design,* No. 15/1966, Tokyo.

IMAI, KENJI
Gaudi and Steiner, in *Glass and Architecture,* No. 3/1964, Tokyo.
Rudolf Steiner and his Works, Kindaikenchiku 5, Tokyo, 1964.
Augenzeuge der modernen Architektur. Schweiz 1926. *Shinkenchiku,* July 1971, Tokyo.

KAYSER, FELIX
Architektur heute und morgen, Verlag Die Kommenden, Freiburg, 1969.

KEMPER, CARL
Der Bau, Verlag Freies Geistesleben, Stuttgart, 1966.

MEISSNER REESE, ILSE
Steiner's Goetheanum at Dornach, in *Progressive Architecture,* September 1965, New York.

MENSCH UND BAUKUNST
Journal edited by Wolfgang Gessner, Felix Durach, Felix Kayser and Erich Zimmer. The Journal appeared between 1951 and 1974.

MESSINA, VITTORIO LETI
Studi sul architettonico di Rudolf Steiner, L.U. Japaore Editore, L'Aquila 1976.

PEHNT, WOLFGANG
Expressionist Architecture, Thames and Hudson, London, 1973.

RAAB, REX
Rudolf Steiner und die Baukunst, in *Bauwelt,* No. 7/1964, Berlin.
Eurythmie und Mysteriendramen im Goetheanum zu Dornach, in *Bühnentechnische Rundschau,* 1/1965, Berlin.
Bedeutung und Aufgabe der Farbe im Schulbau, in *Das Deutsche Malerblatt,* No. 19/1969, Stuttgart.
Möbel für Menschen am Beispiel Tisch und Stuhl, in *Der Deutsche Schreiner,* No. 11/1969, Stuttgart.
Architecture – Buildings for Life, in *Work Arising from the Life of Rudolf Steiner,* Rudolf Steiner Press, London, 1975.

RAAB, REX, ARNE KLINGBORG, ÅKE FANT
Eloquent Concrete. How Rudolf Steiner Employed Reinforced Concrete, Rudolf Steiner Press, London 1979.

RANZENBERGER, HERMANN
Das neue Goetheanum, ein Eisenbetonbau, in *Westdeutsche Bau-Schau*, 1st Dec. 1926.

RATH, WILHELM
The Imagery of the Goetheanum Windows, Rudolf Steiner Press, London, 1976.

ROTZLER, WILLY
Das Goetheanum in Dornach als Beispiel der Integration der Künste, in *Werk*, No. 8/1960, Zurich.

SCHUYT, MIKE, JOOST ELFFERS
Rudolf Steiner und seine Architektur, DuMont Kunsttaschenbuch, Vol. 72, DuMont Verlag, Cologne 1978.

SHARP, DENNIS
Rudolf Steiner and the Way to a New Style in Architecture, in *Architectural Association Journal*, June 1963, London.
Modern Architecture and Expressionism, Longmans Green, London, 1966.
Thoughts of Love in a Concrete Climate, in *The Guardian*, October 1971.

STOCKMEYER, CARL
Der Modellbau in Malsch, Malsch 1969.

TURGENIEFF, ASSYA
The Goetheanum Windows, Rudolf Steiner Publishing Co., London, and Anthroposophic Press, New York, 1938.

WERK
60 Jahre Schweizer Architektur, January 1968, Zurich.

WYSSLING, W.
Zum Neubau des Goetheanums bei Dornach, in *Schweizerische Bauzeitung*, Vol. 85, No. 7.

ZIMMER, ERICH
Rudolf Steiner als Architekt von Wohn- und Zweckbauten, Verlag Freies Giestesleben, Stuttgart, 1970.

Sources of Marginal Quotations by Rudolf Steiner

1907
Luzifer-Gnosis. GA 34, 2nd ed. Dornach 1960. Der Theosophische Kongress in München.

1907/1911
Bilder okkulter Siegel und Säulen. GA 284/285, Dornach 1977.
12.6.1907 Bericht über den Münchner Kongress
Oct. 1907 Zur Einführung
3.1.1911 Die okkulten Gesichtspunkte des Stuttgarter Baues

1911, 12.12.
And the Temple Becomes Man, Rudolf Steiner Press, London 1979.

1914
Ways to a New Style in Architecture, Anthroposophical Publishing Company, London, 1927
17.6. The House of Speech
28.6. The New Conception of Architecture
26.7. The Creative World of Colour

1914
Der Dornacher Bau als Wahrzeichen künstlerischer Umwandlungsimpulse, Dornach 1937.
18.10 Die Formen der Säulen und ihr Zusammenhang mit den Grundimpulsen der Kulturepochen
25.10. Die Malerei der grossen Kuppel

1914
Art in the Light of Mystery Wisdom, Rudolf Steiner Press, London 1970.
29.12. Impulses of Transformation for Man's Artistic Evolution, Lecture Two.

1918/1920
Kunst und Kunsterkenntnis, GA 271, 2nd ed. Dornach 1961
6.5.1918 Die Quellen der Künstlerischen Phantasie
12.9.1920 The Supersensible Origin of the Artistic (in *Art in the Light of Mystery Wisdom*, Rudolf Steiner Press, London 1970).

1918
Die Polarität von Dauer und Entwicklung im Menschenleben. GA 184, 2nd ed., Dornach 1968
21.9. Eighth Lecture.

1919
The Social Future, Anthroposophic Press, New York 1972
28.10. Cultural Questions, Spiritual Science, The Nature of Education, Social Art

1921, 29.6
Der Baugedanke des Goetheanum, 2nd ed., Stuttgart 1958

1923/1924
Die Weihnachtstagung zur Begründung der Allgemeinen Anthroposophischen Gesellschaft 1923/24, GA 260, 3rd ed., Dornach 1963
31.12.1923 Der künftige Baugedanke von Dornach
1.1.1924 Gründungsversammlung (Fortsetzung).

LIST OF ILLUSTRATIONS

	Page
Seventh planetary seal (Seal of Venus)	9
The Munich Congress Hall	10
Jupiter and Venus Capitals	10
The Malsch Model Building – Interior	11
The Column of Jupiter	11
The second seal in the Munich Congress Hall	12
The lecture hall in the Stuttgart House, Landhausstrasse	12
The colonnade in the Stuttgart House, Landhausstrasse	13
"Cosmic Midnight" from a mystery drama by Rudolf Steiner, sketch by H. Kuhn	14
Maria and Johannes Thomasius from a mystery drama by Rudolf Steiner	15
"Ahriman's Realm" from a mystery drama by Rudolf Steiner, sketch by H. Kuhn	15
Model sketch of the Johannes Building in Munich	16
Ground plan of the Johannes Building in Munich	17
Sketches of the columns and architraves	18/19
Rudolf Steiner with a model of the first Goetheanum	20
Rudolf Steiner's interior model of the first Goetheanum	20
Ground plan of the first Goetheanum	22
Interior model of the first Goetheanum	23
Rudolf Steiner on the speaker's rostrum in the carpenters' shop	24
Wood-carving for the first Goetheanum	25
Audience in the carpenter's shop	25
Wood-carving in the first Goetheanum – Saturn Column	26
Members of the architects' office	26
Engraving of the coloured glass windows	27
Window in blue glass	27
The 'Glass Studio'	27
The first Goetheanum under construction	28
Staircase piers	29
Lobby to the Great Hall	30
The first Goetheanum under construction	31
Topping-out ceremony with the workmen	31
Erecting the capitals	32
Column bases, large rotunda	33
Wood-carving on the capitals	33
Capital of the fifth column (Mercury Column)	33
Model of the 'Boiler House'	34
The 'Boiler House'	35
The 'Boiler House' under construction	35
The 'Transformer House'	37
Between the cupolas of the first Goetheanum	38
North wing of the first Goetheanum	38
The concrete substructure of the first Goetheanum	38
West wing of the first Goetheanum	38
Capitals and architraves – model	39
Capital of the sixth column	39
Small rotunda	40
Large rotunda with organ loft	41
Rudolf Steiner at work on the wooden sculpture	43
Model of the wooden sculpture – detail of Ahriman	43
First design for the wooden sculpture	43
The wooden sculpture	43
Model of the wooden sculpture – detail of Ahriman	44
Model of the wooden sculpture – detail of Lucifer	44
The wooden sculpture – detail	44
The centre figure of the wooden sculpture	45
The speaker's rostrum in the 'White Hall'	46
The 'White Hall' in the first Goetheanum	46
The base of the Saturn Column – watercolour by W. Norton	46
Painting in the small cupola	47
'Boiler House' and Goetheanum – watercolour by Hermann Linde	48
The Goetheanum – watercolour by Hermann Linde	48
Eurythmy group	49
The 'Carpenters' Shop Hall' with stage	49
The First Goetheanum	49
Duldeck House from the south-west	50
Duldeck House – south-east entrance	50
Duldeck House – roof in the south-west	50
Duldeck House from the north	51
The first Goetheanum – north terrace	52
The west wing of the first Goetheanum	53
Carpenters during the construction of the first Goetheanum	53
The first Goetheanum	53
The concrete ruin of the first Goetheanum	54
Blackboard sketch by Rudolf Steiner	54
Model for the second Goetheanum	54
Model for the second Goetheanum	57
The west facade of the second Goetheanum	57
Ground plans of the second Goetheanum	57
Southern elevation – second building application	58
The demolition of the first Goetheanum's terrace	58
Alteration to the stage wing	58
The west front – second building application	58
Ground plan at hall level	60
The second Goetheanum under construction	61
Timber form work with steel reinforcement	61
The topping-out ceremony at the second Goetheanum	62
Participants in the topping-out ceremony	62
The Goetheanum freed of its scaffolding	63
The staircase in the west	64

The staircase in the south	64
The attic studio in the south	64
The Goetheanum from the bank of the Birs	65
The Goetheanum from the south-west	65
The Goetheanum from the west	65
The Goetheanum from the north-west	66
Partial view from the north-west	66
Partial view from the south-west	67
The Great Hall at the Goetheanum	69
Blue and violet north windows	69
The Great Hall (unfinished)	70
The staircase in the south	71
The 'Foundation Stone Hall' at ground floor level	72
Cloakrooms on the ground floor	73
The staircase in the west	73
Work model for the west facade	74
The Goetheanum from the south-west	75
Partial view of the south facade	77
Partial views at terrace level	77
West projection from the south	78
Partial view of the western staircase projection	79
North side from the west	80
De Jaager House, models	81
De Jaager House from the north-west	81
De Jaager House from the south-west	82
Wegman House – timber house	82
Schuurman House, west side	82
The Goetheanum, western front	90
Antonio Gaudi, Colonia Güell, Barcelona	92
Peter Behrens, turbine factory, Berlin	92
Walter Gropius and Adolf Meyer, Fagus Works, Alfeld, Leine	93
Max Berg, Centenary Hall, Breslau	93
Bruno Taut, Glass House, 'Werkbund' Exhibition, Cologne	93
Lyonel Feininger, 'The Cathedral of the Future'	94
Title page of the periodical, 'Frühlicht'	94
Wassily Luckhardt, 'City Crown'	95
Hans Poelzig, Grand Theatre, Berlin	96
Erich Mendelsohn, Einstein Tower, Potsdam	96
Paul Gösch, 'Mineral and Organic Architecture'	96
Hermann Finsterlin, 'Bathroom' (sketch)	97
Gerrit T. Rietveld, Schröder House, Utrecht	97
Wladimir Tatlin, project for a monument	97
Le Corbusier, Studio Ozenfant, Paris	98
The Goetheanum, partial view from the south	103
The Eurythmeum, partial view from the north-east	104
The Eurythmeum, models	104
The Goetheanum from the north	108
Alberts, Emmaus Church, Nijmegen	111
Asmussen, Rudolf Steiner Seminariet, Järna	111
Baravalle, Hofmann House, Dornach	112
Bay, Friedwart House, Dornach	112
Billing, Peters and Ruff, teacher training college, Stuttgart	112
Bockemühl, Community Hospital, Herdecke	113
Bowman, Waldorf School, Toronto	113
Devaris and Manteuffel, Michael Hall School, Forest Row	114
Durach, crystallization laboratory, Dornach	114
Griffin, University, Melbourne	115
Gutbrod, Congress Centre, Mecca	115
Hupkes, Church of the Christian Community, Rotterdam	115
Ikehara, cemetery chapel, Tokorozawa	116
Imai, Okuma Memorial Hall, Saga, Japan	116
Jacobson, Lorien Novalis School, Sydney	116
Kayser, villa, Stuttgart	117
Keller, Marwitz House, Dornach	117
Lauer, Church of the Christian Community, Stuttgart	118
Moser, Moser House, Dornach	118
Nemes, Agricultural and Cultural Education Centre, Fulenhagen	119
Ogilvie and Klein, Filder Clinic, Stuttgart	119
Peters, Billing and Ruff, Waldorf School, Stuttgart	119
Podolinsky, kindergarten, Melbourne	120
Pyle-Waller, café and restaurant, Dornach	120
Raab, Church of the Christian Community, Heidenheim	120
Ranzenberger, Weleda AG (first building), Arlesheim	120
Ruff, Peters and Billing, dwelling, Unterlengenhardt	121
Schöpfer, Rosenthal House, Dornach	121
Scholl, Rudolf Steiner House, Pforzheim	122
Seyfert, special home school, Föhrenbühl	122
Tallo, Myrtle Hall, Camphill Village, Aberdeen	122
Tschakalow, curative home school for maladjusted children, 'Arild', Bliestorf	123
Wheeler, Rudolf Steiner House, London	123
Zimmer, Hulton House, Arlesheim	123

ANNOTATIONS

1. Rudolf Steiner, *Bilder okkulter Siegel und Säulen,* 2nd edition, Dornach 1977 (partly published in English in *Occult Signs and Symbols,* Anthroposophic Press, New York 1972).
2. Annot. 1, Page 72.
3. Annot. 1, Page 115.
4. Annot. 1, Page 117.
5. Annot. 1, Page 139 with Annot. Page 182
6. Carl Kemper, *Der Bau,* 2nd edition. Stuttgart 1974, Page 187.
7. Annot. 1, Page 122.
8. G. Gruben/M. Hirmer, *Die Tempel der Griechen,* Munich 1961, Page 193f.
9. Detailed account in Carl Kemper's *Der Bau* (Annot. 6).
10. cp. Georg Hartmann, *The Goetheanum Glass Windows,* Philosophisch-Anthroposophischer Verlag, Dornach 1972.
11. cp. G. Sterner, *Jugendstil.* Cologne 1975, Pages 24f., 38f.
12. Annot. 6, Pages 32, 36.
13. Annot. 1, Page 148.
14. cp. G.C. Argan, *Gropius und das Bauhaus,* Hamburg 1962, Pages 594f.
15. cp. A. Janik and St. Toulmin, *Wittgenstein's Vienna,* New York 1973, Page 252f.
16. Annot. 15, Page 102.
17. Rex Raab, Arne Klingborg and Åke Fant, *Eloquent Concrete,* Rudolf Steiner Press, London 1979.
18. Annot. 17, Page 43.
19. Wolfgang Pehnt, *Expressionist Architecture,* Thames and Hudson, London 1973.
20. Annot. 19, Page 148.
21. Annot. 17, Illustration 29.
22. Annot. 17, Page 41f.
23. Assia Turgenieff, *The Goetheanum Windows,* Rudolf Steiner Publishing Co., London 1938.
24. Annot. 17, Page 63.
25. Annot. 6, Page 23.
26. Annot 17, Page 89.
27. Annot 17, Ill. 99 – 108.
28. 31st year, No. 12, 1952
29. Annot. 17, Page 105.
    Rex Raab, *Le Corbusier und das Goetheanum,* 'Das Goetheanum', 45th year, No. 2, 1966.
30. Annot. 6, Page 19.
    cp. Rex Raab as to the exaggerated ideas which often arise relating to the extent of the reduction in height (Annot. 17), Page 56.
31. Annot. 17, Ill. 30, 34, 35.
32. One might compare the sketch in *Eloquent Concrete* (Annot. 17), Ill. 34, with Ill. 85, or Ill. 30 with Ill. 3, resp. Ill. 35 with Ill. 8 and 11.
33. Annot. 17, Ill. 5.
34. Annot. 17, Page 104, Ill. e.
35. Rudolf Steiner, *Die Weihnachtstagung zur Begründung der Allgemeinen Anthroposophischen Gesellschaft 1923/24,* GA 260, 3rd ed., Dornach 1963.
36. Annot. 17, Ill. 72 – 80.
37. cp. Tom Wolfe, *Das gemalte Wort,* Berlin 1975, Page 6f.
38. Rudolf Steiner *Goethe as Founder of a New Science of Aesthetics,* Anthroposophical Publishing Co, London 1922.
39. Rudolf Steiner, *Psychologie der Künste* (9.4.1921) in 'Kunst und Kunsterkenntnis', Page 172f, in particular Page 176 (Annot. 38)
40. Rudolf Steiner *The Being of the Arts* in '1979 Golden Blade', Rudolf Steiner Press, London.
41. Rudolf Steiner *Anthroposophie, Ein Fragment aus dem Jahre 1910,* GA45, 2nd ed. Dornach 1970, Page 32.
42. Rudolf Steiner *Das Sinnlich-Übersinnliche in seiner Verwirklichung durch die Kunst,* in 'Kunst und Kunsterkenntnis', (Annot. 38).
44. Rudolf Steiner *Die Quellen der künstlerischen Phantasie und die Quellen der übersinnlichen Erkenntnis* in 'Kunst und Kunsterkenntnis' (Annot. 38).
45. Christian Morgenstern *Stufen* (1912), Basle 1977.
46. Rudolf Steiner *The Supersensible Origin of the Artistic* in 'Art in the Light of Mystery Wisdom', Rudolf Steiner Press, London 1970.
47. Annot. 39, Page 172f.
48. A more extensive bibliography of Rudolf Steiner's explanations of art is comprised in:
    Rudolf Steiner, *Das literarische und künstlerische Werk.* Dornach 1961, Page 112f. (Editor: H. Wiesberger).
49. Willy Rotzler, *Das Goetheanum in Dornach als Beispiel der Integration der Künste,* Werk No. 8/1960, Zurich.
50. Erich Zimmer, *Rudolf Steiner als Architekt von Wohn- und Zweckbauten,* Stuttgart 1970.
51. Kenji Imai, *Eye-Witness of Modern Architecture,* Switzerland 1926, Shinkenchiku, July 1971, Tokyo.
52. Dennis Sharp, *Rudolf Steiner and the Way to a New Style in Architecture,* Architectural Association Journal, June 1963, London. *Modern Architecture and Expressionism,* London 1966; *Thoughts of love in a concrete climate,* The Guardian, October 1971.
53. Ilse Meissner-Reese, *Steiner's Goetheanum at Dornach,* Progressive Architecture, September 1965, New York.
54. Yuji Agematsu, *Achitecture as a Philosophy of Life: Rudolf Steiner,* Tokyo 1974 (Japanese).
55. Yuji Agematsu, *Rudolf Steiner, the Artist,* Tokyo 1978 (Japanese).
56. From the first publication of the Johannes Building Association, Munich 1911: An die Mitglieder der Theosophischen Gesellschaft, Deutsche Sektion und deren Freunde. Der Verwaltungsrat des Johannesbau-Vereins.

Rudolf Steiner Press

35 PARK ROAD LONDON NW1 6XT

RUDOLF STEINER'S SCULPTURE IN DORNACH

Ake Fant, Arne Klingborg, A. John Wilkes

Rudolf Steiner's wood sculpture of the 'Representative of Humanity' — or the 'Christ Being' as he himself also referred to it — is a unique work of art, and this book seeks to introduce it to a wider public than has hitherto been possible. Not only does it contain a fine series of photographs of the sculpture which have not been previously published, but with the aid of many more pictures of the various plasticine and wax models, provides an intriguing survey of its development. These are supported by a factually clear and artistically perceptive commentary as well as by numerous clearly documented utterances of Rudolf Steiner's on his own conception of the work and its particular style of execution.

translated by A. J. Wilkes and E. Westerberg
Rudolf Steiner Press, 1st edition, London 1976
ISBN 0 85440 301 9 (cloth)
23.6 × 30.2 cm   with 72 plates   88 pp.

THE GOETHEANUM GLASS-WINDOWS

Georg Hartmann

The glass windows of the Goetheanum building pose numerous questions to the visitor concerning their forms, colours, and motif. It is the aim of this booklet to try and answer these questions. The booklet contains 12 coloured plates and many black and white photographs and illustrations.

translated by I. Zeindler
Philosophisch-Anthroposophischer Verlag, 1st edition
Dornach 1972 (paper)
13.5 × 22 cm   76 pp.

THE IMAGERY OF THE GOETHEANUM WINDOWS
An interpretation in verse form

Wilhelm Rath

In these verses, Wilhelm Rath has given expression to his experience of the windows of the first Goetheanum. The folder also contains nine separate colour plates of these windows, which were designed by Rudolf Steiner.

translated by W. Mann
Rudolf Steiner Press, 1st edition, London 1976
ISBN 0 85440 300 0 (folder)
22.3 × 32.6 cm   with 9 separate colour plates   32 pp.

COLOUR

translated by J. Salter
Rudolf Steiner Press, 3rd edition, London 1977
ISBN 085440 310 8 (paper)
13.8 × 21.6 cm   with 3pp. colour illustrations   96 pp.